ABSOLUTE SCIENCE

Pupil Book 1

Collins

Brian Arnold • Geof... ...ones • Emma Poole

Published by HarperCollins*Publishers* Limited
77–85 Fulham Palace Road
Hammersmith
London
W6 8JB

Browse the complete Collins catalogue at
www.collinseducation.com

© HarperCollins*Publishers* Ltd 2002
Reprinted 2003, 2005

10 9

ISBN-13 978 0 00 713586 8

British Library Cataloguing in Publication Data
A Catalogue record for this publication is available
from the British Library

Commissioned by Martin Davies
Edited by Margaret Shepherd
Design and Project Management by AMR Ltd.
Covers by Chi Leung
Illustrations by Art Construction, Josephine Blake,
Mik Brown, Phillip Burrows, Chartwell Illustrators,
Belinda Evans, David Woodroffe.
Production by Jack Murphy
Printed and bound by Printing Express, Hong Kong

**Every effort has been made to contact the
holders of copyright material, but if any have
been inadvertently overlooked the publishers
will be pleased to make the necessary
arrangements at the first opportunity. The publishers would like to thank the following for
permission to reproduce photographs (T = Top,
B = Bottom, C = Centre, L= Left, R = Right):**

John Adds, 22B, 24, 26, 29;
P J Adds, 28;
Allsport UK/M Powell, 104T, A Bello, 104B, T
Lewis, 105L, M Thompson, 105R;
© Amblin Entertainment, picture from: The Ronald
Grant Archive, 181B;
Arab Potash Company, 132;
Bill Butland, ARPS, 9;
Martyn Chillmaid, 6BL, 7CR, 10C, 11B, 18TL, TR,
C&B, 35, 36, 40, 41, 59R, 76, 101, 146;
Bruce Coleman Ltd/J Burton, 51, H Reinhard, 57T;
Corbis/B Battersby, Eye Ubiquitious, 10T, D Jones,
95R;
Format Photographers/J O'Brien, 56CL, J
Chapman, 56BR, U Preuss, 57B, M Reik, 59L,
159;
John L E Gaisford, 102;
Gettyimages, 103, 108L, 110, 128;
Geoff Jones, 114, 138;
Andrew Lambert Photography, 6TR, 88, 129R&L,
137;
Frank Lane Photo Library/S Maslowski, 120, L
West, 162;
NASA, 175;
NHPA/A Ackerley, 39;
Natural History Museum, London, 161;
Oxford Scientific Films Ltd/I Cushing, 48;
Science Photo Library/G Garradd, 7TR, M Kulyk,
16, Dr J Burgess, 22T, F Lercy, 52, NASA, 55, F
Sauze, 84, 172, C D Winters, 95TL&BL, 108R, J-L
Charmet, 154, Tom van Sant Geosphere Project,
170, P Parviainen, 171R, L Landolfi, 171L, Rev. R
Reyer, 177L, Prof. J Pasachoff, 177R, M Garlick,
180, B Bachman, 181, J Sanford, 182, F Zullo,
183, E Slawick, 184;
Margaret Shepherd, 18BR&CL, 129C, 145;
Skyscan/Caroline Claughton, 11T&C;
Still Pictures/P Frisch-Muth, 70L, F Dott, 70R, N
Dickinson, 73, Klein/Hubert, 75;
Woodfall Wild Images/D Woodfall, 43.
Cover Image: *Vibrio cholerae* Science Photo
Library/Hans-Ulrich Osterwalder.

Contents

1 The particle model of solids, liquids and gases

Look around the room you are in. Everything you can see is made of **matter**. There are three different kinds of matter. These are **solids**, **liquids** and **gases**. We use the **properties** of a material to help us decide whether a material is a solid, a liquid or a gas.

1 Choose ten objects or materials from the above diagram. Then decide if they are solids, liquids or gases. Put your answers in a table similar to the one shown below.

Solid	Liquid	Gas

2 Under your table write down one sentence for each of the ten objects, explaining why you think it is a solid, a liquid or a gas.

3 Where in your table would you put the following:

   a toothpaste   **b** sand   **c** glass   **d** jelly?

   Why is it quite difficult to decide which groups these materials belong to?

Why are solids, liquids and gases different?

Ancient man had many different ideas about matter.

Whose ideas were correct?
How did the scientists decide?

A detective trying to solve a crime he did not see, will gather together as much information as possible so that he can make some sensible guesses. Based on these guesses he will look for further evidence to confirm his ideas.

A good guess based upon some sensible ideas is called a **hypothesis**. If we then discover lots of evidence that seems to support this guess, our idea then becomes a **theory**.

Scientists carry out their experiments and investigations in a similar way. Having looked at all the evidence, they came to the conclusion that:

• the particle theory of matter was the correct one
• the particles in solids, liquids and gases are arranged differently
• the particles in solids, liquids and gases move about differently,

Can you suggest what evidence these scientists look at?
What evidence can we gather so that we can draw our own conclusions?

Gathering the evidence

What evidence do we have to help us decide how the particles are arranged?

Solids

YOU MAY BE ABLE TO DO WORKSHEET A1, 'DENSITY OF A MATERIAL'.

This desk and stool are made from solids. They have their own shape and are strong.

It is very difficult to squash most solids. They are incompressible.

You may be able to do Worksheets A2, 'Growing crystals' and A3 'Splitting crystals'.

This weight is made from a solid. A small amount of it weighs a lot. It is **dense**.

These crystals of copper sulfate all have the **same shape**.

4 Copy these sentences and choose the correct word to complete them.

  a Solids are (easy/hard) to compress.
  b Solids have a (high/low) density.

Liquids

Liquids are **not strong**. They will not support this boy.

Liquids can be poured. They can **flow**.

Liquids have **no shape of their own**. They take the shape of the container into which they are poured.

Liquids can not be squashed they are **incompressible**.

Liquids are **dense**. A small amount of them weighs a lot. Have you tried to pick up two buckets filled with water?

Although water takes the shape of the container into which it is poured, water droplets have a round, almost spherical, shape

5 Copy these sentences and choose the correct word to complete them.

  a Liquids (can/cannot) flow.

  b Liquids (do/do not) have a fixed volume.

Gases

Gases are easy to squash. They can be **compressed**.

Gases have a **low density**. Large volumes of gases weigh very little.

Gases fill the whole of this balloon.

6 Copy these sentences and choose the correct word to complete them.

    a Gases have a (low/high) density.

    b Gases (do/do not) have a fixed volume.

Now that we have had a look at some of the differences between solids, liquids and gases, let's see if we can build a **particle model** for each.

Let's look first at some of our evidence and see how it helps us decide *how* the particles are arranged in solids, liquids and gases.

Solids

Evidence	Model
Most solids cannot be squashed. Most solids are quite dense.	These suggest that the particles are close together.
Solids have their own shape. Solids can be strong.	These suggest that the particles are in fixed positions and held together by strong forces.
The crystals of a solid usually all have the same shape.	This suggests that the particles are arranged in a pattern.

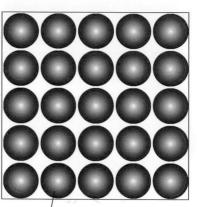

The particles are close together and form a regular pattern.

Particle model for a solid.

Liquids

Evidence	Model
Liquids are still quite dense but slightly less dense than solids. Liquids cannot be squashed.	These suggest that the particles are still close together but not as close as they are in a solid.
Liquids have no shape of their own and can flow.	This suggests that the forces between particles are weaker than the forces between the particles in a solid. They allow the particles to slide over each other.
Water droplets have round surfaces.	This suggests that there are still some forces between the particles in a liquid.

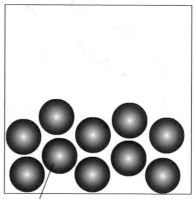

The particles are still quite close together, but there is no regular pattern.

Particle model for a liquid.

Gases

Evidence	Model
Gases have very low density. Gases are very easy to squash.	These suggest that the particles in a gas have lots of empty space between them.
Gases fill completely any container into which they are placed.	This suggests that there are no forces holding the gas particles together.

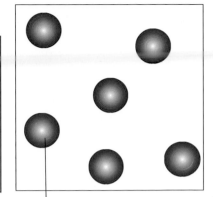

The particles are well spread out and are in all parts of the container.

Particle model for a gas.

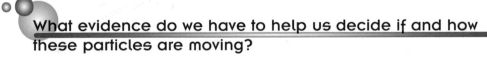

7 Copy and complete these sentences.

   a _____ have their own shape.

   b _____ are easy to compress.

   c _____ do not have their own shape, but do have a fixed volume.

   d _____ and _____ are hard to compress.

What evidence do we have to help us decide if and how these particles are moving?

Solids

YOU MAY BE ABLE TO DO WORKSHEET A4, 'EXPANSION AND CONTRACTION OF SOLIDS'.

These railway tracks increased in length as they were warmed by the Sun. They **expanded**. The engineers who built the railway line forgot to leave any **expansion gaps** so the tracks buckled. These days the tracks are constructed in a different way, and expansion gaps are no longer needed.

YOU MAY BE ABLE TO DO WORKSHEET A5, 'EXPANSION AND CONTRACTION OF METALS'.

As Concorde flies, friction with the air causes its temperature to increase and it expands. When it is flying at supersonic speeds, it is approximately 30 cm longer than it is on the ground.

8 Is the Eiffel Tower taller in the summer or the winter?

Liquids

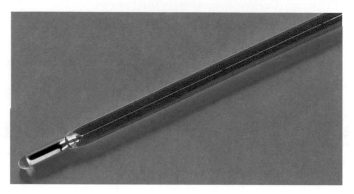

As the liquid mercury in this thermometer becomes warm, it expands and rises up the tube. As it cools, it contracts and the column of mercury becomes smaller.

9 What is unusual about the metal mercury?

| Ink added to water | After 15 minutes | After 30 minutes |

YOU MAY BE ABLE TO DO WORKSHEET A6, 'DIFFUSION IN LIQUIDS'.

Even without stirring, the ink added to this water will gradually spread out and mix with the water. This mixing is called **diffusion**. If the experiment is repeated using warm water and warm ink, the mixing takes place more quickly.

10 Why can blackcurrant squash turn a whole glass full of water red, even though it is not stirred?

Gases

As the air in this balloon is heated it expands and fills the balloon.

The smell of this air freshener will quickly reach all parts of the room. Gases, like liquids, spread out and mix but they do it more quickly.

You may be able to do Worksheet A7, 'Brownian motion'.

If we put too much air inside a balloon it will burst. This happens because the air pressure inside the balloon is too great for the material that the balloon is made from.

11 Copy this sentence and choose the correct word to complete it. When a gas is cooled it (expands/contracts).

Now let's see how we can use all of this evidence to decide how the particles in our models behave.

Solids

Evidence	Model
When solids are heated they **expand**. When solids are cooled they **contract**.	These suggest that as solids are heated, their particles become warm and vibrate more vigorously. The particles need more space and so move further apart. These suggest that as solids are cooled, their particles vibrate less vigorously. The particles need less space and so move closer together.
Solids placed in contact with each other do not mix.	This suggests that although the particles in a solid can vibrate, they have fixed positions from which they cannot move.

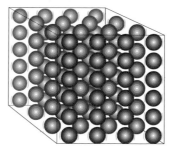

In a solid the particles are close together, in a pattern and vibrating.

Liquids

Evidence	Model
When liquids are warmed they expand. When they are cooled they contract.	This suggests that the particles vibrate more vigorously when warm and less vigorously when cool.
When two liquids are put into the same container, they can mix without stirring.	This suggests that the particles in a liquid do not have fixed positions. They are moving around.
The warmer the liquids, the more quickly they mix.	This suggests that the warmer the particles, the faster they move around.

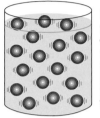

In a liquid the particles are still close together, but not in a regular pattern. The particles can move past each other – they can flow.

Gases

Evidence	Model
When gases are warmed they expand. When cooled they contract.	This suggests that the particles move around more quickly when warm and more slowly when cool.
When two gases are put into the same container, they mix very quickly even without stirring.	This suggests that the particles in a gas do not have fixed positions and are moving around very quickly.
Gases exert pressure.	This suggests that the particles in a gas are continually colliding with the sides of its container. These collisions create **pressure**.

In a gas the particles are spread out and move about very quickly.

Testing our models

If our models of solids, liquids and gases are good models, we should now be able to use them to explain other properties and behaviour. Can you explain any of these?

Why, with a sharp blade, is it possible to cut a crystal and produce two flat faces and yet in other directions the crystal will not cut? It may shatter instead.

Why is the hot water in a liquid always at the top?

Why, when air is taken out of a plastic bottle, might the bottle collapse?

Changing state

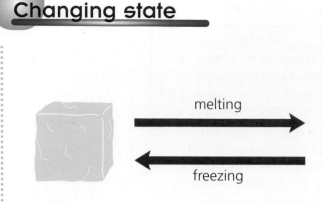

melting

freezing

If solid ice is heated, its particles vibrate more vigorously. Eventually the particles vibrate so much that the regular structure breaks down and the particles are able to move past each other. The solid ice has changed into liquid water.

The temperature at which a solid melts to become a liquid is called the **melting point** of the solid.

If a liquid is cooled it will freeze to form a solid. The temperature at which a liquid does this is called the **freezing point** of the liquid.

12 What is the melting point of water?

13 What is the freezing point of water?

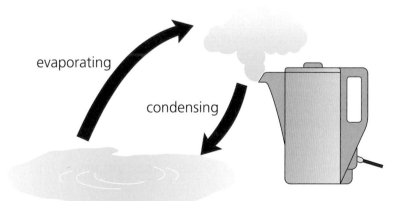

evaporating

condensing

If liquid water is heated, the vibrations of its particles will become more violent and eventually its particles will become completely free. The water has changed into a gas or vapour. The temperature at which this happens is called the **boiling point** of water. If the water vapour is cooled, it will **condense** to form liquid water.

This diagram summarises all the evidence we have gathered about changes of state and particle movement.

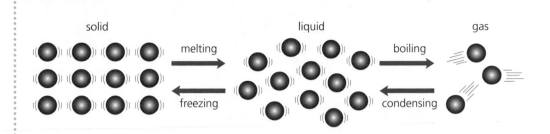

Different substances have different melting points and boiling points.

Substance	Melting point (°C)	Boiling point (°C)
water	0	100
lead	328	1755
iron	1539	2900
oxygen	−219	−183

14 Is lead a solid, a liquid or a gas at: **a** 25°C   **b** 1000°C?

15 Is oxygen a solid, a liquid or a gas at: **a** −250°C   **b** 10°C?

16 Is water a solid, a liquid or a gas at: **a** −5°C   **b** 95°C?

Snowflakes

Snowflakes have fascinated people for hundreds of years. Seen under a microscope, every snowflake is **unique** – no one has ever found two flakes that are exactly the same!

In Britain most of our rain begins its downward journey as snow, but melts as it falls. Only when the air temperature is so cold that the flakes can reach the ground without melting, do we actually see it snowing.

In 1611 a scientist called Johannes Kepler discovered that every snowflake had six sides. He could not explain why this was, but hypothesised that it must be to do with the way that the ice particles are joined together. It was more than three centuries later that Kepler's questions were finally answered. Using a technique called X-ray crystallography, scientists could see how the particles inside the snowflake were arranged. They found that the particles were arranged in a regular pattern which gave every snowflake six sides.

a What does the word unique mean? Give an example of a unique object.

b When do we actually see it snow?

c What did Johannes Kepler discover about snowflakes?

d Why was Kepler unable to prove that his ideas were correct?

e What technique enabled scientists to confirm how the particles are arranged in a snowflake?

f How are the particles arranged in crystalline solids?

Key ideas

Now that you have completed this chapter, you should know:

- that materials can be classified as solids, liquids or gases
- that solids, liquids and gases have different properties
- that all materials are made up of particles that are too small to see
- that these particles are arranged differently in solids, liquids and gases
- that these particles move differently in solids, liquids and gases – this is why solids, liquids and gases have different properties.

Key words

boiling point	liquid
compressible	matter
condense	melting point
density	particle model
diffusion	pressure
expand	property
expansion gap	shape
flow	solid
freezing point	strength
gas	theory
hypothesis	unique
incompressible	

1 Copy and complete these sentences.

   a The **particles in a solid** are _____ together. They can _____ , but cannot move around freely. So solids have a fixed _____ and _____ .

   b The **particles in a liquid** can _____ more freely. Liquids have a fixed _____ but not a fixed _____ .

   c The **particles in a gas** move very _____ and in all _____ . Gases do not have a fixed _____ or _____ .

2 Draw diagrams to show how the particles are arranged in:

   a a solid

   b a liquid

   c a gas

Explain how the particles are moving in each of the three states.

3 Design a key that could be used to identify whether a material is a solid, a liquid or a gas. Then use your key to classify the materials shown below.

End of chapter questions

4 Decide whether the following statements are true or false.
  a Solids have a fixed shape.
  b Gases can flow.
  c Liquids and solids both have a fixed volume.
  d Gases fill any container into which they are released.
  e Liquids can be compressed easily.
  f Gases are less dense than solids.
  g A substance exists as a gas if its temperature is below its freezing point.
  h When a gas condenses it changes into a liquid.
  i The particles of a liquid are completely free to move around.

5 Give an everyday example of:
  a a solid turning into a liquid
  b a liquid turning into a gas
  c a liquid turning into a solid

6 The letters of the following words have been jumbled up. Un-jumble the letters and write one sentence to explain what each of these words means.
  a wolf   e idfofnusi   i riplseatc
  b udilqi   f sag   j snedceno
  c pomcinlisbesre g ssethypoih   k rhoyet
  d tedysin   h pinaxenos   l legmint

7 Draw a poster to show water particles can exist as a solid, a liquid and a gas.

8 Write an essay describing a world in which only two states of matter exist. You can choose which two.

9 Do some research to discover the meanings of the following words.
    atom   molecule   element   compound   sublimation

10 Make a summary of everything you have learned about in this chapter. Your summary could be in the form of a spider diagram or flow diagram or even as bullet points – it is entirely up to you, but your piece of paper must be no larger than a postcard.

What are living organisms made of?

Anna woke up in the night. She had a horrible pain around her middle and was very sick. She tried really hard to go back to sleep, but the pain kept her awake and she was sick again. In the morning, her mum took her to hospital to see what was wrong. The doctor who examined her said she had appendicitis and would need an operation straight away to remove her appendix. Several hours later, Anna felt much better. When her surgeon visited her, he answered some of her questions.

'What is an appendix? Why did you have to take it out? Where is it now?', asked Anna one after the other. The surgeon smiled and answered, 'Your appendix is an organ in your digestive system. It had become infected and inflamed. That is why you were in so much pain. So we decided to remove it. And here it is!'.

That's one of my organs!

Organs

Your body contains many different parts. These parts are called **organs**. Plants and animals, are made up of different organs. Usually, each organ has a particular task or **function** that it carries out. The appendix is unusual because it is of no use to us. It does not have a function.

The diagrams opposite show some organs in a plant and a human. Do you know what they all are?

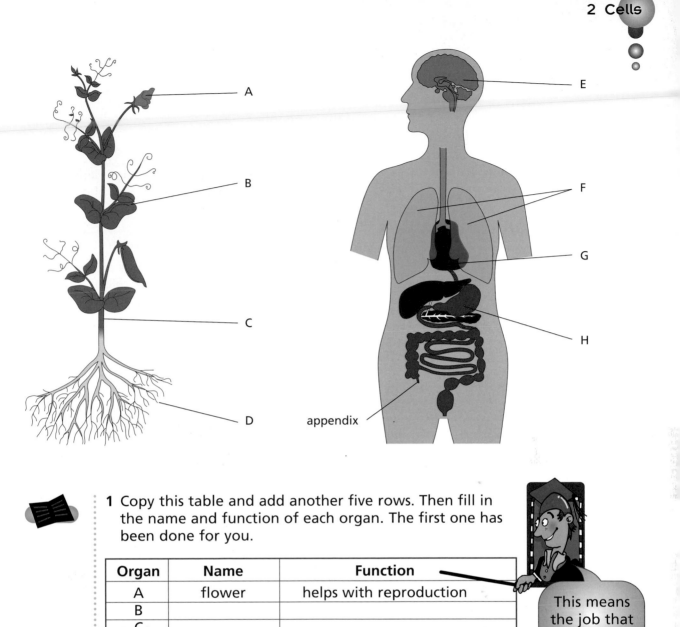

A

B

C

D

E

F

G

H

appendix

1 Copy this table and add another five rows. Then fill in the name and function of each organ. The first one has been done for you.

Organ	Name	Function
A	flower	helps with reproduction
B		
C		

This means the job that the organ does.

What are organs made of?

If animals and plants are made up of organs, then what do you think organs might be made of?

No-one knew the answer to this question until magnifying lenses and microscopes were invented. This happened in the seventeenth century.

Soon, many people who were interested in the world around them had bought a lens or a microscope. Robert Hooke, an English scientist, was one of these people. In 1665, he cut some thin slices from a piece of cork. He looked at the cork slices through his microscope.

Hooke saw that the cork was made up of lots of tiny boxes. He called these boxes **cells**. He wrote a book about the things he had seen with his microscope. The book included this drawing of what he saw.

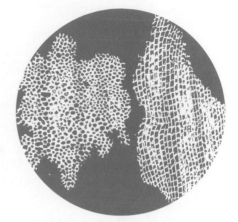
Robert Hooke's drawing of cork cells.

As time went on, the design of microscopes got better and better. People could see small things more and more clearly. Today, we have microscopes that allow us to see really tiny things very clearly.

These photographs show some different parts of different organisms, seen through a microscope. Can you see what they all have in common?

Part of a pondweed leaf.

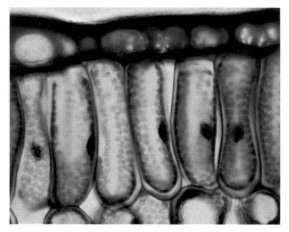
Part of a sunflower leaf.

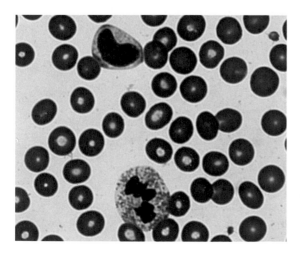
Human blood.

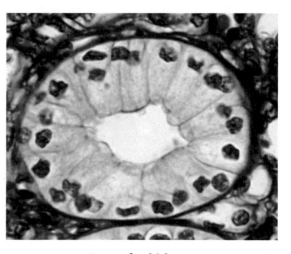
Part of a kidney.

You can probably see that all of these parts are made up of 'boxes' – like Hooke's piece of cork. Throughout the seventeenth century, many different scientists looked at many different parts of plants and animals. No matter what they looked at, they always saw that it was made of tiny 'boxes'. Because Hooke had called these boxes cells, everyone else used that word too.

Eventually, by 1839, two German scientists, Schleiden and Schwann, decided that all living things must be made up of cells. This is sometimes called the **cell theory**.

Using a microscope to look at cells

YOU MAY BE ABLE TO DO WORKSHEET B1, 'USING A MICROSCOPE'.

Cells are very small, so if you want to see them you have to use a microscope.

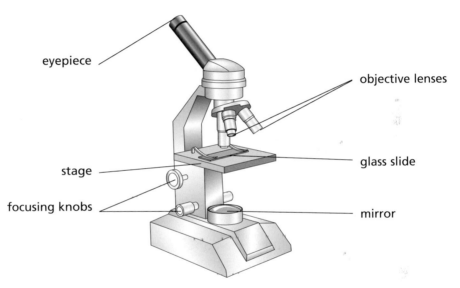

The parts of a microscope.

YOU MAY BE ABLE TO DO WORKSHEETS B3 'LOOKING AT PLANT CELLS' AND B4 'LOOKING AT ANIMAL CELLS'.

The piece of animal or plant that you want to look at is called the **specimen**. You will need to put it on a small piece of glass called a **slide**. Usually, an even smaller piece of glass, called a **cover slip**, is put on top of the specimen, to hold it in place. The slide is then put onto the stage of the microscope.

Light from a lamp is reflected by the mirror through the slide and then through the microscope's lenses. When you look down the microscope, you see a magnified image of part of the specimen.

Why does a specimen that you want to look at through a microscope need to be very thin?

The photographs and drawings show what some of these cells might look like.

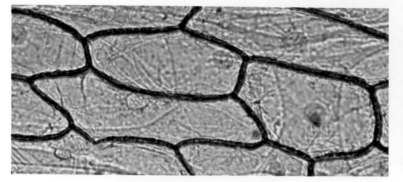

Photograph of onion cells.

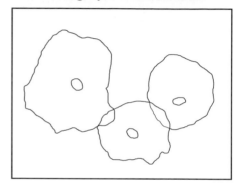

Photograph of cheek cells.

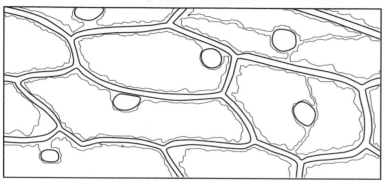

Drawing of onion cells.

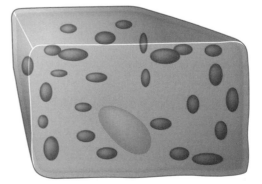

Drawing of cheek cells.

The structure of cells

These diagrams show what an animal cell and a plant cell look like. The first diagram of each pair shows what the whole cell might look like.

The second diagram shows what it would look like if you sliced it in half through the middle. This is called a cross-section. We usually draw diagrams of cells like this, because then we can show all the things inside them much more clearly.

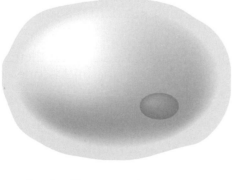

An animal cell as seen from the outside.

A plant cell as seen from the outside.

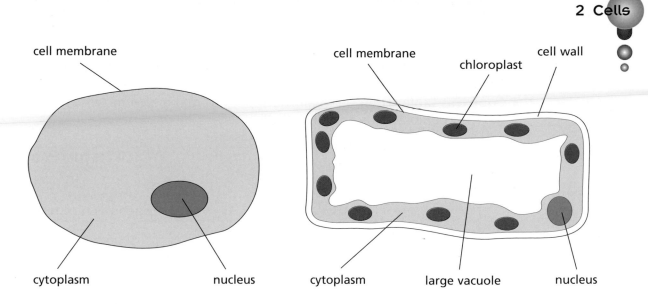

An animal cell as a cross-section.   **A plant cell as a cross-section.**

Most of a cell is made up of a watery, jelly-like substance called **cytoplasm**. Cytoplasm isn't usually coloured, so it can be difficult to see. If you worked through Worksheet B4 and looked at some of your cheek cells, you probably added a blue stain to them. The cytoplasm soaked up this stain, so it looked blue. The cytoplasm is where all the reactions happen that keep the cell alive.

You may have been able to see a darkish spot inside the cells that you looked at under a microscope. This is called the **nucleus** of the cell. Almost all cells have a nucleus. The nucleus controls what the cell does.

All cells have a **cell membrane**. This is an extremely thin layer all around the outside of the cell. It is very delicate and flexible, rather like the skin on a soap bubble. The cell membrane has a very important function – it controls what is allowed to go in and out of the cell.

Plant cells have something which no animal cell ever has. They have a strong **cell wall** all around them. The cell wall is made of millions of tiny, criss-crossed fibres of a substance called **cellulose**. The cell wall helps to hold the cell in shape, and stops it bursting if a lot of water seeps into the cell.

Many plant cells have a large space inside the cytoplasm called a **vacuole**. The vacuole is filled with a liquid, called **sap**. The sap contains substances that the plant cell may need to survive, such as sugars.

Some plant cells contain green structures called **chloroplasts**. Chloroplasts look green because they contain a green substance called **chlorophyll**. Chlorophyll absorbs energy from sunlight. This energy is used by the plant cell to make food. This process is called **photosynthesis**.

A scientist once said that a plant cell is like an animal cell in a box. Do you think that is a good description?

2 Why do you think the onion cells that you looked at don't have chloroplasts?

3 Copy this table. Then fill in all the spaces to make a comparison between animal cells and plant cells.

Part of cell	Do animal cells have it?	Do plant cells have it?	What is its function?
cytoplasm	yes	yes	This is where reactions happen.
nucleus			
cell membrane			
cell wall			
vacuole			
chloroplast			

4 Which of these photographs show animal cells, and which show plant cells? How can you tell the difference?

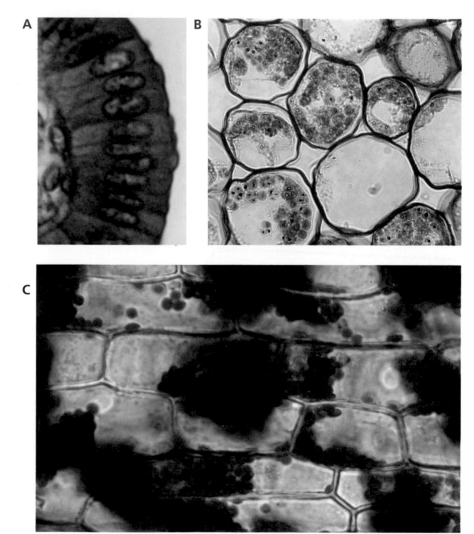

Special kinds of cells

You have already seen many different kinds of cells. Imagine how many different sorts there must be in all the different kinds of living organisms in the world!

You know that all animal cells have a nucleus, cytoplasm and a cell membrane. Even so, they can still be very different from one another.

In a human, there are many different kinds of cells, each with a particular function to carry out. Each kind of cell is said to be **specialised** for its function. Here are some examples.

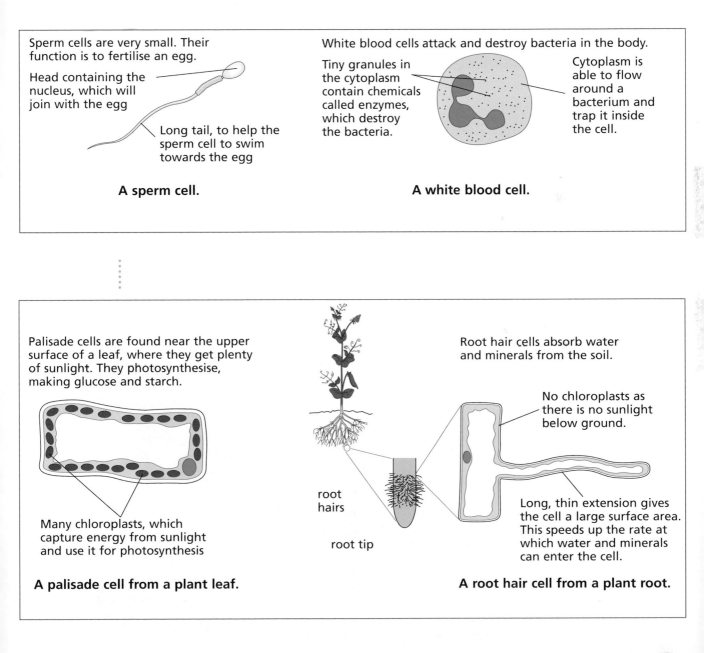

Sperm cells are very small. Their function is to fertilise an egg.

Head containing the nucleus, which will join with the egg

Long tail, to help the sperm cell to swim towards the egg

A sperm cell.

White blood cells attack and destroy bacteria in the body.

Tiny granules in the cytoplasm contain chemicals called enzymes, which destroy the bacteria.

Cytoplasm is able to flow around a bacterium and trap it inside the cell.

A white blood cell.

Palisade cells are found near the upper surface of a leaf, where they get plenty of sunlight. They photosynthesise, making glucose and starch.

Many chloroplasts, which capture energy from sunlight and use it for photosynthesis

A palisade cell from a plant leaf.

Root hair cells absorb water and minerals from the soil.

No chloroplasts as there is no sunlight below ground.

root hairs

root tip

Long, thin extension gives the cell a large surface area. This speeds up the rate at which water and minerals can enter the cell.

A root hair cell from a plant root.

Do you think an elephant has bigger cells than a human? Or, do you think elephant cells are the same size as human cells, but there are more of them? How could you find out?

Cells, tissues and organs

A plant leaf is an example of an organ, and it is made up of cells. If you look at a leaf edge on, you might think there is only room for one layer of cells. However, the cells are so tiny that there is actually room for several layers.

The yellow patch on this holly leaf is where a tiny insect larva, called a leaf miner, has burrowed between the top and bottom layers of the leaf. It has eaten the cells inside.

There are several different kinds of cells in a leaf. If you cut a very thin slice out of a leaf and looked at it under a microscope, it would look like this.

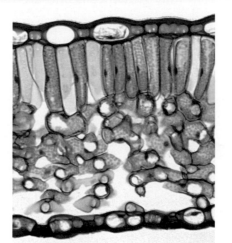

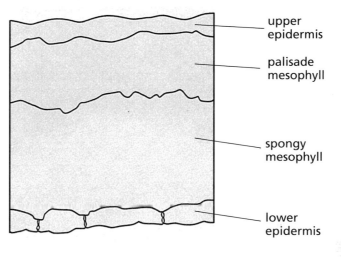

- upper epidermis
- palisade mesophyll
- spongy mesophyll
- lower epidermis

This drawing shows the different tissues in the leaf.

5 How many different kinds of cells can you see in the leaf?

6 Which cells can make food by photosynthesis? How can you tell?

You can see that the different kinds of cells are not just scattered anywhere. They are arranged in layers, with similar cells together.

For example, all of the cells on the surface of the leaf are quite thin, and they don't have chloroplasts. Just beneath them is a layer of tall, thin cells with chloroplasts. And underneath those is a layer of more rounded cells with big spaces between them.

Each of these groups of cells is called a **tissue**. A tissue is a group of similar cells which are all carrying out the same function. Each organ in a plant or a human is made up of different tissues, all containing specialised cells grouped together, for example, the skin, the brain and the liver.

Where do new cells come from?

New cells come from fully grown cells and are made when older cells divide into two.

This diagram shows how a cell divides into two.

An animal cell about to divide.

The nucleus has divided.

The cell is beginning to divide.

The cell has divided.

How an animal cell divides.

7 Which part of the cell divides first?

8 What do you think has to happen to the two new cells before they will be able to divide again?

YOU MAY BE ABLE TO DO WORKSHEET **B10**, 'INVESTIGATING CELLS IN FILAMENTOUS ALGAE'.

Whenever a cell divides, it is always the nucleus that divides first. You know that the nucleus controls what the cell does. The nucleus contains information that tells the cell what to grow into and what to do. So it is absolutely essential for each new cell to get a complete set of this information.

Just before the cell divides, the information in the nucleus is copied. So now there are two full sets of this information. When the nucleus divides, one complete set of information goes into each new nucleus. So, when the whole cell divides into two new cells, each one gets all the information it needs to tell it to grow and behave in the right way.

New skin for burns victims

Jack was badly burned when he was nine years old. This is what he said about how it happened.

'Well, I was playing with matches. I was sitting on a 250 litre tank of fuel. The next thing I knew I was engulfed in flames.'

Jack's legs were very badly burned. There was not much skin left on them. Apart from being very painful, this is very dangerous. Without skin, there is nothing to stop the cells underneath from drying out and dying. Also, it is easy for bacteria to get in and cause infections.

Usually, if you cut or graze your skin, the skin cells around the wound divide to form new ones. The new cells spread out over the wound and stick together to form new skin tissue. But, if the burn is very deep and very widespread, then the skin cells that are left can't cope with this. Even when they do manage to make new skin, it takes a very long time. So people with bad burns are often given skin grafts. Small pieces of skin are taken from other parts of their body, and put onto the wound.

Now a new way of producing new skin is being used. A few of the patient's own skin cells are removed. They are put into a warm solution containing all the nutrients they need. They grow and divide, grow and divide, forming a new sheet of skin. They can produce a piece of skin 200 times the size of the sample taken from the patient in about three or four weeks. This skin is sometimes known as tissue-engineered skin. It can then be placed over the burned areas, where it forms a new layer of protective skin.

Jack's burns were treated with tissue-engineered skin. He does have scars, but he says, 'At least I still have my legs, even if they aren't pretty.'

a Explain why deep and widespread burns may threaten a person's life.

b Suggest why skin grafting is often impossible if a person has widespread burns.

c Why do you think the skin produced by the new technique is said to be 'engineered'?

d Suggest two reasons why the new technique is likely to save more lives than the old skin grafting method.

Key ideas

Now that you have completed this chapter, you should know:

- that plants and animals are made of organs, that organs are made up of tissues and that tissues are made up of cells

- how to use a microscope, how to prepare slides for viewing with a microscope, and how to make clear drawings of what you can see using a microscope

- how Robert Hooke and other scientists helped to increase our knowledge about cells

- what plant and animal cells look like, and the important similarities and differences between them

- the functions of the cell membrane, cytoplasm, nucleus, cell wall, chloroplasts and vacuoles in a cell

- about how the structure of some specialised cells – such as sperm cells, white blood cells, root hair cells and palisade cells – adapts them for their functions

- that new cells are formed by the division of fully-grown cells

- that cell division always begins with the division of the nucleus.

Key words

cell	nucleus
cell membrane	organ
cell theory	photosynthesis
cell wall	sap
cellulose	slide
chlorophyll	specialise
chloroplast	specimen
cover slip	tissue
cytoplasm	vacuole
function	

1 Copy and complete these sentences.

   a Organs are made up of _____ , which are made up of cells.

   b Both animal and plant cells are surrounded by a _____

      _____ .

   c Plant cells also have a _____ _____ around the outside of them.

2 Write a sentence describing the function of each of these organs in a human.

     an eye   the heart

3 Write a sentence describing the function of each of these organs in a plant.

     flower   leaf

4

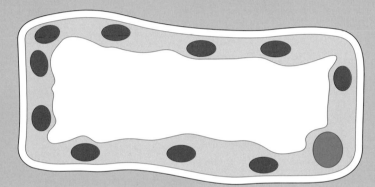

Copy or trace this diagram of a plant cell.

Use a pencil and ruler to draw label lines to each of these structures, and label them.

    nucleus   cytoplasm   vacuole   cell membrane   cell wall

5 Name three structures which are found in plant cells but never in animal cells.

6 Name the part of a cell which has each of these functions.

   a Controls what goes into and out of the cell

   b Stores sugars and other substances, in a liquid called cell sap

   c Contains chlorophyll and carries out photosynthesis

   d Controls the activities of the cell

7 Draw three or four diagrams to show what happens when a cell divides.

8 Make a poster to illustrate either:

     the structure of a plant cell and what each part does,

     or the differences between animal and plant cells

9 Find out about the structure of viruses, and what they do. Write at least two paragraphs explaining why they are unusual, and why some people do not think they are living things.

3 Acids and alkalis

Acids and alkalis are two types or groups of chemicals. We meet and use both of these types of chemicals everyday of our lives. There are even some of these chemicals inside you!

Everyday acids

Juices in your stomach, which digest the food you have eaten, contain an acid called **hydrochloric acid**.

Fruits such as apples, oranges and lemons contain acids.
Citrus fruits contain an acid called citric acid.
It is the acid inside a fruit which gives it a sharp, sour taste.

Car batteries contain a strong acid called **sulfuric acid**.

Vinegar contains an acid called acetic acid.

Sour milk contains lactic acid.

The bite from an ant contains formic acid. It is the acid which makes the bite sting or itch.

Everyday alkalis

Oven cleaners, washing up liquids and soaps all contain alkalis.

Alkalis help to remove and dissolve grease.

Alkalis have a soapy feel because they dissolve the grease on your skin.

Toothpaste contains alkalis.

Indigestion medicines contain alkalis.

The word 'alkali' is unusual and comes from the Arabic word for ashes (al kali). Early Arabs dissolved ashes in water to make alkaline solutions that were very good for cleaning things.

1 a Name the acid found in your stomach.
 b Why do lemons taste sour?
 c Name the acid found in car batteries.
 d Where is lactic acid found?
 e Why do ant bites itch?

2 a Name three alkalis you could find in your school kitchen.
 b Why do alkalis make your skin feel slimy?
 c How did alkalis get their unusual name ?

3

How many acids and alkalis can you spot in this diagram?
Try to find out the names of the acids and alkalis you have spotted.

4 All these foods
 contain acids.
 Name the acid in
 each case. Put your
 answers in a table
 like the one below.

Food	Acid
vinegar	acetic acid

Being safe

Some chemicals are dangerous and must be used with great care. They are marked or labelled with hazard symbols, which tell us how they can harm us.

 corrosive

 toxic

 oxidising

 harmful

 irritant

 highly flammable

To be safe we must pay attention to hazard signs and understand what they mean.

5 Draw the hazard symbol for:
   a harmful
   b irritant
   c corrosive

Lorries transporting chemicals must display hazard signs even when the chemicals are harmless. This lorry is carrying a strong acid. This information is shown by the hazard symbols. The symbols also explain how the chemical should be dealt with in an emergency.

6 a Why must a lorry display hazard signs even when the chemicals it is carrying are harmless?

b Why are there no hazard warnings on lemons and vinegar?

7 a If you spilt an acid on your hand in the laboratory, what would you do?

b If you dropped a bottle of sulfuric acid, how could you make the area safe?

Safety rules

It is important to work safely with chemicals such as acids and alkalis. Look at these pairs of students. They have different ideas about how to work safely. Try to decide in each case who is right. Can you explain why?

Now write a list of rules for using acids and alkalis, the first one is done for you.

Rules for using acids and alkalis

1 When using acids or alkalis always wear goggles.

2

3

4

Is it an acid or an alkali?

Red beetroot   **Green grass**

Beetroot is red and grass is green because they contain chemicals called dyes. Some of these dyes change colour if an acid or an alkali is added to them. We can use these changes in colour to test if a chemical is acidic or alkaline. We are using these dyes as **chemical indicators**.

The acid/alkali bush

In soil which is alkaline the dye in the petals of this hydrangea is pink.

In soil which is acidic the dye changes colour and the petals are blue.

YOU MAY BE ABLE TO DO WORKSHEET C1, 'MAKING INDICATORS'.

Using Indicators

The table below shows the colours of a range of indicators in different solutions.

A **neutral** solution is one which is neither acidic nor alkaline.

Indicator	Acid	Neutral	Alkali
methyl orange	red	yellow	yellow
red litmus	red	red	blue
blue litmus	red	blue	blue
phenolphthalein	colourless	colourless	pink

YOU MAY BE ABLE TO DO WORKSHEET C2, 'TESTING INDICATORS'.

Methyl orange is red in acidic solutions.

Litmus paper turns blue in alkaline solutions.

8 a What colour is red litmus in an alkali?
  b If methyl orange is added to an acid solution, what colour would you see?
  c If blue litmus is added to an alkaline solution what colour would you see?
  d What colour is red litmus in a neutral solution?

Universal indicator

One of the most useful indicators is **universal indicator**. It consists of a mixture of dyes which produces a range of colours which tells us not only if a solution is acid or alkali, but *how* acidic or *how* alkaline the solution is.

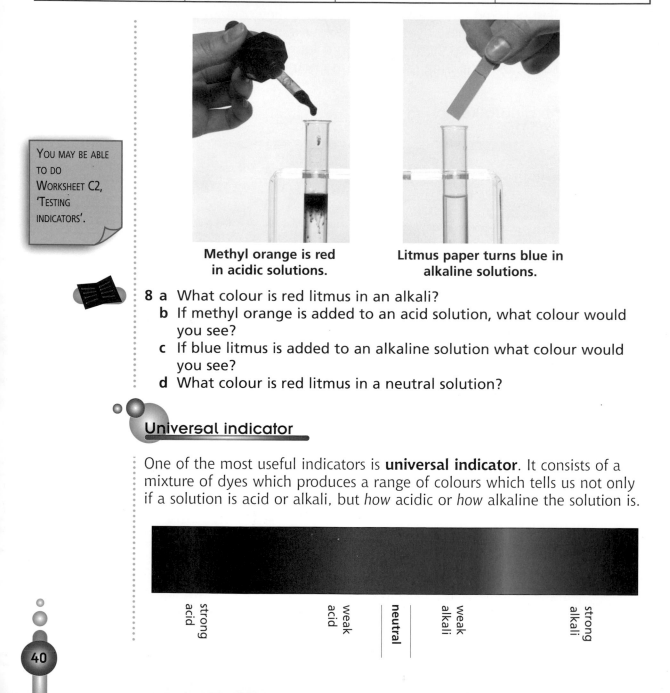

strong acid   weak acid   neutral   weak alkali   strong alkali

YOU MAY BE ABLE TO DO WORKSHEET C3, 'TESTING UNIVERSAL INDICATOR'.

Universal indicator paper turns blue in alkaline solutions …   **… and red in acidic solutions.**

The pH scale

We also use a numbered scale to indicate the strength of a solution. It is called the **pH scale**.

If a solution is neutral it has a pH value of 7.

Solutions that are acidic have pH values which are less than 7.

Solutions that are alkaline have pH values that are above 7, up to a maximum value of 14.

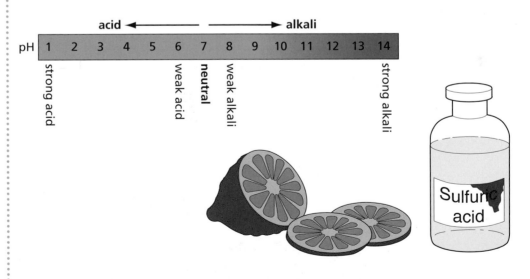

Strong acids and strong alkalis are dangerous. The bottles in which they are kept should display hazard symbols. Very weak acids and alkalis are safe to use in everyday situations and therefore do not need to have hazard symbols.

9 a What is the pH of a neutral solution?
  b What is the pH range for an acidic solution?
  c What is the pH range for an alkaline solution?

10 Two solutions are tested: one has a pH of 2, the other a pH of 6. Which is the stronger acid?

11 a What is the pH of a strong alkali?
  b What is the pH of a weak alkali?

Neutralisation

Have you ever been stung by a bee or a wasp?

If you have, you will know it isn't a very pleasant experience – but do you know what to do to treat the sting?

When a wasp stings, it pumps an alkaline solution into the skin. If you rub vinegar onto the area, you can balance out the alkali which causes the pain. So, you will soon feel a lot better.

When a bee stings, it uses an acidic solution to irritate the skin. If you rub an alkaline solution like camomile, or a solution of baking soda into the area, you can balance out the acid and stop the sting hurting.

This balancing out of an acid with an alkali, or an alkali with an acid, is called **neutralisation**.

12 a Why are wasp and bee stings different?
  b How should you treat a wasp sting?
  c How should you treat a bee sting?

Neutralising soils

The farmer in the photograph above has tested his soil and found that it has become very acidic. Most crops only grow well if the soil has a pH value that is near to neutral. The farmer is therefore adding lime to his soil. Lime is alkaline and will neutralise the acid in the soil.

13 a Suggest how the farmer might have tested his soil to find its pH value.
  b Why does a farmer want the soil to have a pH around 7?
  c If the soil is too acidic, what can a farmer do?
  d What will happen to the pH of the soil if lime is added?

Treating indigestion

Neutralisation is also used to treat **indigestion** in people.

This boy has eaten too many green apples. They have made his stomach produce lots of acid and he now has indigestion.

Indigestion can be cured by eating **antacid** tablets (antacids are alkaline). The antacid neutralises the extra acid, so you feel better.

14 a What causes indigestion?
  b What is an antacid?
  c How do antacids work?

Acid rain

Acid rain has been a major environmental concern for several decades, but its full effects are only just being understood.

Acid rain is formed when fossil fuels like coal and oil are burnt. These fuels contain sulfur. When the <u>fuel</u> is burnt the sulfur forms sulfur dioxide, a gas which can cause asthma, headaches and coughs. When the sulfur dioxide is released into the atmosphere, it dissolves in rain water to form acid rain.

The acid rain attacks limestone buildings and statues. It can also speed up the <u>corrosion</u> of metals. In 1967 forty-six people were killed when a bridge over the Ohio river collapsed because of corrosion caused by acid rain. Forests are also seriously affected. Acid rain washes away essential <u>nutrients</u> from the soil near the trees' roots. Sometimes the trees die very quickly. At other sites, the trees become weak and die later when they are attacked by pests such as beetles.

One of the worst affected areas are lakes. The acid rain enters the lakes as rain, snow, sleet or hail and changes the pH of the water. In many areas, the worst time is spring when nearby snow melts and a lot of acidic water runs into the lake. This causes a terrible and dramatic change in the pH of the lake. The animal life in the lake has no time to adapt to this sudden change. Spring is also the time when many insects, fish and <u>amphibians</u> lay eggs in the water to hatch. The drastic change in the pH of the water can deform or kill these young creatures.

However, we can all do something to reduce acid rain. Much of the coal and oil which is burnt is used to generate electricity. If we turn off lights when they are not in use, and only fill the kettle with the water we need, we can all do something to reduce the problems of acid rain on our <u>environment</u>.

a Explain the meaning of the words that have been underlined.
b How is sulfur dioxide formed?
c Explain how sulfur dioxide can form acid rain.
d How does acid rain damage trees?
e Why is spring the worst time of year for an animal that lives in a lake affected by acid rain?
f Give two ways that *you* can reduce the amount of acid rain that is produced.

Key ideas

Now that you have completed this chapter, you should know:

- some of the hazards of acids and alkalis, and how to deal with such hazards
- the names of some common acids, such as hydrochloric acid and vinegar
- the names of some common alkalis such as sodium hydroxide and bleach
- that acids and alkalis are found in many everyday situations
- that many foods contain acids, while many cleaning materials contain alkalis
- that indicators are chemicals that change colour when added to acidic or alkaline solutions
- that pH values can also be used to classify a solution as acidic, neutral or alkaline. Acids have a pH less than 7. Neutral solutions have a pH of 7, and alkaline solutions have a pH of more than 7
- that if equal amounts of acid and alkali are mixed, a neutral solution is formed which has a pH of 7. This type of reaction is called neutralisation
- that wasp stings are alkaline and can be treated by rubbing an acidic solution like vinegar into the skin
- that soils which are too acidic to grow a certain crop can be neutralised by adding lime to them.

Key words

acid	irritant
alkali	litmus
antacid	neutral
chemical indicator	neutralisation
corrosive	oxidising
flammable	pH scale
harmful	sulfuric acid
hydrochloric acid	toxic
indigestion	universal indicator

1 Rearrange the following anagrams, then write out the word and its description.

a daci   A solution with a pH value of less than 7. The chemical opposite of an alkali.

b lakail   A solution with a pH value of more than 7. The chemical opposite of an acid.

c tacnirido   A chemical that changes colour when placed in an acidic, neutral and alkaline solution.

d tranitsaunoeli   The reaction between equal amounts of acid and alkali which gives a neutral solution with a pH of 7.

e visorceor   A chemical that attacks other tissue including skin and eyes.

f ganpHer   A scale used to measure whether a solution is acidic, neutral or alkaline.

2

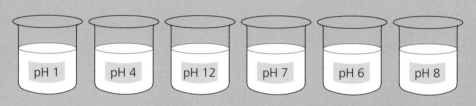

Copy these six diagrams into your book. The label on each beaker shows the pH of the solution it contains.
Colour each beaker to show the colour you would see if you added universal indicator to that beaker.

3 Copy and complete these sentences.

a Some _____ like vinegar and fruit juice can be found in your school canteen. These two acids are safe to handle, we can even eat them. Acids have a _____ taste.

b Other _____ like battery acid are more dangerous . If you are working with this acid you must protect your eyes by wearing _____ .

c Indicators work by changing _____ when placed in acidic, neutral or alkaline solution.

4 Copy and complete these sentences.

   a Alkalis are the chemical opposites of _____ .

   b Many household cleaning products like _____ contain alkalis.

   c If you spill an alkali on your hand it feels _____ .

5 The table below shows six solutions. Each solution has been tested using universal indicator, red litmus and blue litmus.
The pH of each solution is shown. Copy the table and complete the three columns to show the colour you would expect to see.

Solution	pH	Colour with universal indicator	Colour with red litmus	Colour with blue litmus
A	7			
B	2			
C	8			
D	6			
E	12			
F	1			

6 Draw a poster to show some everyday uses of neutralisation.

4 Reproduction

How does a new life start?

There is a pond in Joe's garden. The pond is very quiet during the winter but, in late February, the pond suddenly comes to life. It fills up with frogs, all splashing about and croaking noisily.

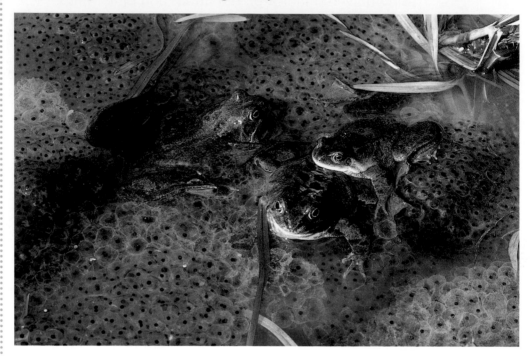

Many of the frogs cling together in pairs. The male frogs hold tightly onto the much larger, fatter female frogs. Each female lays hundreds of soft, round eggs. As the eggs leave her body, the male frog squirts sperms onto the eggs.

Soon, the pond is full of frog spawn. Over the next few days, Joe can see the black blob in the centre of each egg slowly changing, until it has turned into a small black tadpole. The tadpoles usually hatch some time in March, but this depends on the weather. If it is cold, it takes them longer.

Fertilisation

For many animals, a new life starts when an egg is **fertilised** by a sperm. The nucleus of the sperm cell fuses with the nucleus of the egg cell. The new cell which is formed by fertilisation is called a **zygote**. The zygote then divides over and over again to form a new baby organism made up of thousands of cells.

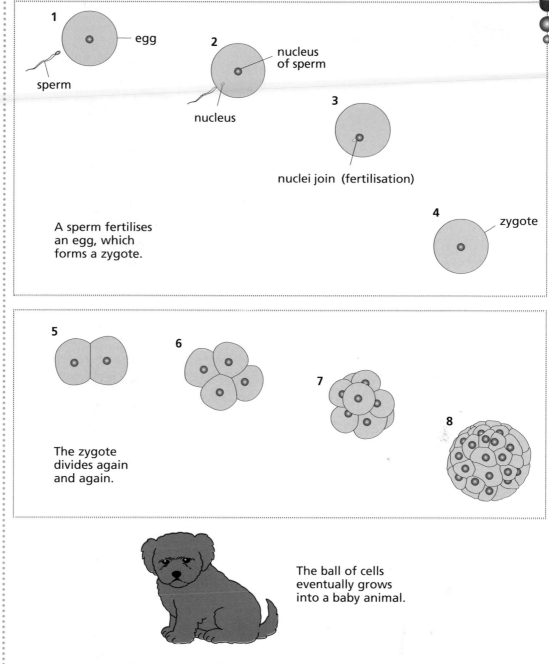

1 egg

2 nucleus of sperm

sperm

nucleus

3

nuclei join (fertilisation)

A sperm fertilises an egg, which forms a zygote.

4 zygote

5

6

7

8

The zygote divides again and again.

The ball of cells eventually grows into a baby animal.

Fertilisation and the development of a baby animal.

The frogs in Joe's garden pond release their eggs and sperms into the water. The sperms fuse with the eggs in the water, not inside the female frog. This is called **external fertilisation**. ('external' means 'outside') Fish also use external fertilisation.

For animals that live on land, external fertilisation wouldn't work very well – the eggs and sperms would just dry up on the ground. So, land-living animals usually keep the eggs inside the female's body. The male animal puts sperms into her body, and the sperms swim to find the eggs and fertilise them. This is called **internal fertilisation**. ('internal' means 'inside') All mammals and birds use internal fertilisation.

1 Here is some information about the numbers of eggs that are produced at any one time by some female animals.

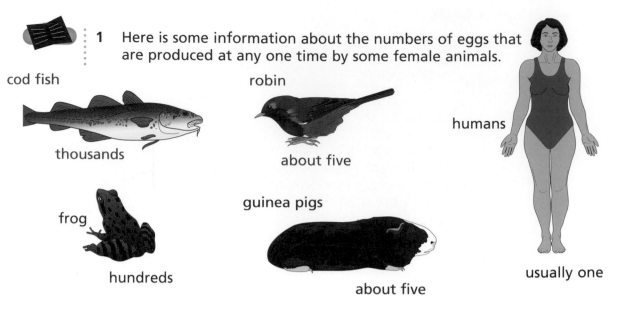

cod fish
thousands

robin
about five

humans
usually one

frog
hundreds

guinea pigs
about five

a Which of these animals use external fertilisation and which use internal fertilisation?

b Think about how easy it will be for a sperm to find an egg. When will this be easier – with external fertilisation or with internal fertilisation?

c Think about how safe the eggs are. Will they be safer with external fertilisation or with internal fertilisation?

d Use your answers to **a**, **b** and **c** to explain the differences in the number of eggs produced by these five animals.

Development

Once the tadpoles have hatched, they have a very dangerous life. Almost everything in the pond seems to eat tadpoles! Fish, newts, dragonfly larvae, water beetles, pond skaters and water boatmen all love tadpoles for lunch. Tadpoles will even eat each other if they can't find anything else to eat!

The tadpoles will take several months to grow into adult frogs and become ready to leave the pond. By this time, there will be only a few left – all the rest will have been eaten.

Joe also keeps guinea pigs. When he wants more guinea pigs, he puts the male in the same cage as the female for a few days. They mate, and some of the female's eggs are fertilised inside her body.

Guinea pigs are mammals. Mammals have a special way of producing young. The zygotes (fertilised eggs) stay inside the female's body while they grow and develop. Here they are warm and safe. The developing young get everything that they need to live from their mother – you can read more about this on page 54. A few weeks after mating, the female guinea pig gives birth to her babies. There are often five or six of them.

 2 Can you think of another reason why fish and frogs produce many more eggs than guinea pigs and humans?

How humans reproduce

Humans are mammals. Like all mammals, we use internal fertilisation. The baby develops inside the mother's body. After birth, the baby is cared for by its parents until it is ready to lead an independent life.

The human reproductive organs

These diagrams show the structure of the reproductive organs of (a) a woman and (b) a man.

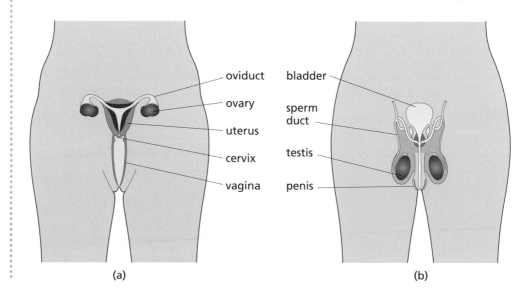

(a)　　　(b)

Eggs, sperms and fertilisation

Each part of the male and female reproductive organs has its own special function.

The eggs are made in the **ovaries**. In an adult woman, one egg leaves one of the ovaries about once each month. This process is called **ovulation**.

An egg is about the same size as a full stop. It moves into the **oviduct**. The inside of the oviduct is covered with microscopic 'hairs' called **cilia**. The cilia wave in time with one another, sweeping the egg along the oviduct towards the **uterus**. The egg moves slowly, so this takes several days.

The sperms are made in the **testes**. In an adult man, thousands of sperms are made each day. During mating, the man inserts his **penis** into the woman's **vagina**. The sperms, mixed with some fluid, travel along the sperm duct and through the penis. They emerge from the penis at the top of the vagina, just next to the **cervix**.

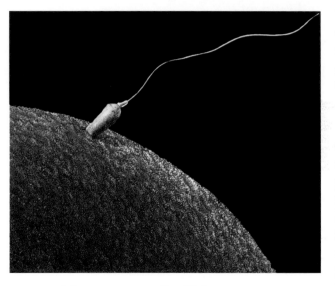

A human sperm fertilising an egg (greatly magnified).

The tiny sperms now have to work hard to try to find the egg. It is a long way to the oviduct for the tiny sperm cells, and most of them will never get there. Only the strongest, fittest sperms will make it all the way.

If there is an egg in one of the oviducts, then the first sperms to arrive cluster around it. They all push at it with their pointed heads, trying to break in. Only one sperm will succeed and push its head into the cytoplasm of the egg. The sperm's head contains chemicals called **enzymes** that help to dissolve a pathway for the sperm. A tough covering immediately forms around the egg, stopping any more sperms from getting in.

Now the nucleus of the sperm fuses with the nucleus of the egg. The egg has been fertilised and has become a zygote. A new human life has begun.

3 These sentences describe the journey of a sperm from where it is made to when it successfully fertilises an egg. Work out the order of the events and copy them down in the correct sequence.

  A They arrive in the oviduct.

  B They travel along the sperm duct and through the penis.

  C Here one sperm fertilises the egg.

  D They swim from the vagina through the moisture in the uterus.

  E The sperms are made in the testes.

4 Divide about one quarter of a page into two columns:

Sperm cell	Egg cell

Now write each of these descriptions into the correct column.
Take care – some descriptions need to be written in *both* columns!

Contains a nucleus.

Has a cell membrane.

Is much smaller than most cells.

Is much larger than most cells.

Has only a small amount of cytoplasm.

Has a large amount of cytoplasm.

Has a tail to help it to swim.

Has a head containing enzymes to help it to push into the egg.

Contains food reserves in its cytoplasm.

If you have time, you can add a drawing of a sperm cell and an egg cell to your table.

Pregnancy

While the baby is developing in her uterus, a woman is said to be **pregnant**. In humans, pregnancy lasts for about nine months.

You will remember that the egg was fertilised in the oviduct. Now it is a zygote. It moves on along the oviduct – still being swept along by the cilia – all the way to the uterus. This can take a couple of days. While it is travelling, the zygote starts to divide. First it splits into two cells, then four, then eight – eventually forming a little ball of cells. The ball of cells is called an **embryo**. This is how everyone's life begins.

1 An egg is fertilized in the oviduct. A zygote is formed.

2 The cells in the zygote keep dividing as it moves into the uterus. It is now an embryo.

3 The embryo sinks into the soft lining of the uterus.

4 It grows a connection with the uterus called the placenta.

What happens to a fertilised egg.

On arrival in the uterus, the embryo sinks into the thick, soft lining of the uterus wall. Up to now, it has only had the food stores in the egg to survive on. Now, it grows a connection to the uterus wall, called the **placenta**. Inside the placenta, the blood of the mother comes very close to the blood of the growing and developing embryo. It is the growing baby's life-support system. The placenta is linked to the embryo by the **umbilical cord**.

Placenta facts

- *The placenta is a round, flat structure that connects a developing embryo to its mother.*

- *It is an unusual organ because it is made partly by the embryo and partly by the mother. It is one organ belonging to two different organisms!*

- *It grows as the embryo grows. By the time the baby is born, the placenta has a diameter of about 12 cm and is 3 cm thick.*

- *Inside the placenta, the blood of the mother and the baby flow beside each other, so that substances can pass from one to the other.*

- *The mother's and baby's blood do not mix. If they did, and they were of different blood groups, then one sort could make the other go lumpy – this would be very dangerous.*

- *The baby's lungs and digestive system are not working yet, so oxygen and nutrients (food substances) pass from the mother's blood into the baby's blood.*

- *The baby's waste substances, including carbon dioxide, pass from the baby's blood into the mother's blood.*

- *After the baby is born, the placenta separates from the uterus wall and passes out through the vagina. Because this happens just after the baby is born, the placenta is sometimes called the afterbirth.*

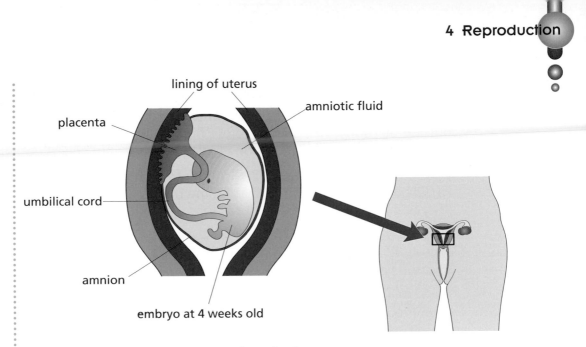

lining of uterus

amniotic fluid

placenta

umbilical cord

amnion

embryo at 4 weeks old

An embryo in the uterus.

When he is space-walking, this astronaut is linked to the spacecraft by an umbilical. Why is it called this?

The amnion

A protective bag grows around the embryo, called the **amnion**. The amnion fills with fluid, and this helps to support and protect the embryo. It is rather like its own private, warm, protective pond.

The cells in the embryo carry on dividing, over and over again. All the different kinds of specialised cells, tissues and organs are formed by about eleven weeks after fertilisation, and the embryo is then called a **fetus**. By that time, it is about 70 mm long – a person in miniature.

Birth and afterwards

After spending nine months in its mother's uterus, the baby is ready to live outside her body. A few days before birth begins, the baby usually turns over so that its head is facing downwards.

The strong muscles in the wall of the mother's uterus begin to contract. First, the contractions gradually pull the opening of the cervix wider. Then they begin to push the baby down through the cervix and the vagina into the outside world.

Although the contractions are not very painful to begin with, they can become very uncomfortable towards the end of the birth. The mother can be given strong painkillers to help her.

Birth is a difficult time for the baby, too! After being in a warm, protected place suddenly the baby is in the world by itself. It takes its first breath, and light shines into its eyes for the very first time. No wonder new-born babies cry!

A baby is immediately responsive to the world around it.

But the baby is not, of course, alone. All mammals take care of their young, and humans do this for longer than any other animals. Another very special thing about mammals is that the mother's body produces **milk** for the baby to feed on in the first few months of its life. Animals which are not mammals do not do this.

The mammary glands of this mother cat produce milk to feed her babies.

Milk and babies are made for each other. The mother's milk contains all the things that a baby needs, in just the right amounts – so it is the perfect diet! It also contains chemicals called **antibodies**. They help to defend the body against bacteria and viruses which can cause disease. When it is very young, a baby's immune system is not fully developed, so it is very useful for the baby to be able to 'borrow' some antibodies from its mother until it can make them for itself.

Can you think of some reasons why mothers may not always want to breast-feed their babies?

How do humans change as they grow?

It takes many years for a baby to grow into an adult person and there are several stages of development that we go through from birth to old age.

Babyhood. A baby is unable to feed itself and needs a lot of care from its parents.

Childhood. A young child is able to talk, walk, run and feed itself.

Adolescence. During adolescence, a person grows rapidly. The sex organs develop.

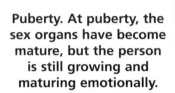

Puberty. At puberty, the sex organs have become mature, but the person is still growing and maturing emotionally.

Adulthood. No further growth takes place during adulthood, but a person's brain continues to learn and mature.

Old age. As a person ages, some functions of the body become less efficient.

Growth

Throughout the first four of these stages, that is from babyhood to puberty, the person grows. Like most mammals, we stop growing when we reach adulthood.

We grow because cells in our bodies grow and then divide to form more cells. We each began life as a single cell – a zygote. By the time we have reached adulthood, we are each made up of about many thousand million cells.

Why are we all different from each other and yet still similar to each other?

The sperm and egg carry information in their nuclei which is then copied into each cell in the new person. So, we inherit some of our characteristics from our mother and some from our father.

Identical twins are produced when one egg is feritilised by one sperm, then splits to form two zygotes. Each twin has identical genes.

Non-identical twins are produced when two different eggs are fertilised by two sperms. Two different zygotes are formed. The twins have different genes.

We do not grow steadily, nor do we all grow in the same way. People are all shapes and sizes. Life would be rather boring if we were all the same!

Most people have two definite 'growth spurts'. You can see them on this graph. The growth spurts are when the line is going up most steeply.

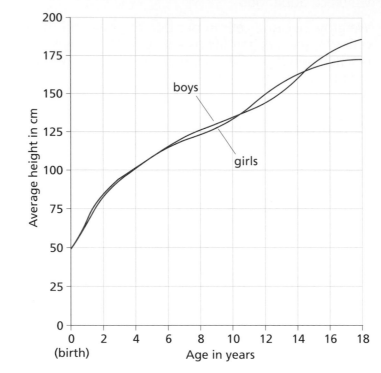

This graph shows the average height of boys and girls between birth and 18 years old.

YOU MAY BE ABLE TO DO WORKSHEET D8, 'HOW TALL ARE THE PEOPLE IN MY CLASS?'

5 At which ages do the growth spurts happen? Are they the same for boys and girls?

Development

We do more than just grow bigger as we get older. Many changes take place in the structure and functions of the body. These changes are called **development**.

The biggest change in the body comes at around the ages of ten to fifteen. During this time, the reproductive organs begin to become active. This stage in a person's life is called **adolescence**. By the time adolescence is over, the person is said to have reached **puberty**. The age at which this happens varies quite a lot from person to person. In general, it tends to happen earlier for girls than for boys, but this is not always the case.

The changes that happen during adolescence are caused by **hormones**. Hormones are chemicals that are produced in the body, and are carried all around it in the blood. The hormones that cause the changes during adolescence are sometimes called **sex hormones**. They are produced by the ovaries in a girl, and by the testes in a boy.

In a girl, the breasts develop and the hips widen. Periods (menstruation) begin.

In a boy, the voicebox gets larger and the voice breaks. The testes and penis grow. Shoulders and chest broaden.

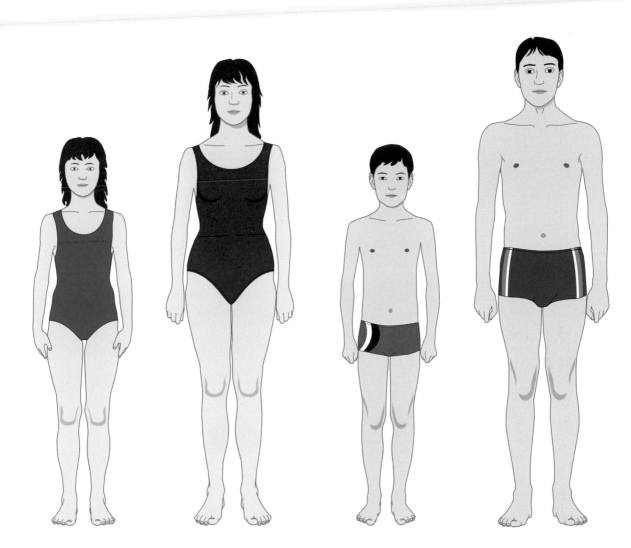

During adolescence in both girls and boys, the body grows rapidly. Pubic hair begins to grow.

Menstruation

One of the biggest changes that are brought about by these sex hormones in a girl's body is that her ovaries begin to release an egg every month. Each time an egg is released, the soft lining of the uterus grows thicker, ready to receive a zygote if the egg is fertilised. If the egg is not fertilised, then the uterus lining slowly breaks down and is gradually lost through the vagina. This is called a **period** or **menstruation**. After menstruation, the lining slowly builds up again, ready for the next egg that will be released from an ovary.

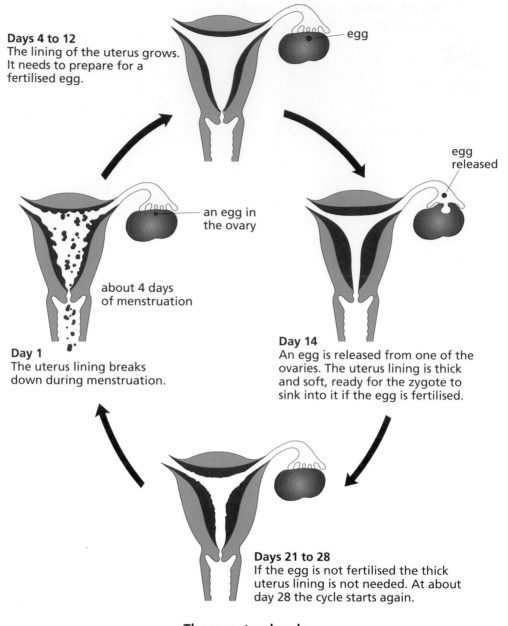

Days 4 to 12
The lining of the uterus grows. It needs to prepare for a fertilised egg.

egg

Day 1
The uterus lining breaks down during menstruation.

an egg in the ovary

about 4 days of menstruation

egg released

Day 14
An egg is released from one of the ovaries. The uterus lining is thick and soft, ready for the zygote to sink into it if the egg is fertilised.

Days 21 to 28
If the egg is not fertilised the thick uterus lining is not needed. At about day 28 the cycle starts again.

The menstrual cycle.

Most adult women have a period once each month, lasting between five and seven days. But, like everything to do with human beings, not everyone is the same! Some women have periods more often than this, while some have them less often. For some women, their periods can be painful, because the muscles in the uterus and abdomen contract strongly, causing unpleasant cramp-like pains. A woman can get special pain-killers from her doctor if this becomes a real problem.

Test tube babies

Some women are not able to become pregnant. Sometimes, this is because their oviducts are blocked.

One way of helping a woman with blocked oviducts to become pregnant is to use a technique called 'in vitro' fertilisation. Most people use the term 'test tube fertilisation' to describe this technique. It is quite expensive, costing about £2000 to £3000.

First, the woman is given hormones that cause her ovaries to produce lots of eggs. She is given an anaesthetic, and some of these eggs are collected from her ovaries using a thin needle. The eggs are put into a dish, in a liquid which provides them with substances they need to keep them alive. Sperms are collected from her partner, and added to the dish. The sperms fertilise some of the eggs.

The eggs are inspected using a microscope, and two or three of those that have been fertilised are placed inside the woman's uterus. Hopefully, at least one of them will grow into a baby and be born in the usual way.

The younger the woman is, the more likely it is that this technique will work. For women less than 35 years old, it works about 45 times out of 100. Between 35–40 years old, it is about 32% successful, whereas for women over the age of 41 it is only 3% successful.

a Explain why a woman cannot get pregnant if her oviducts are blocked.
b Suggest why lots of eggs are collected from the woman, and not just one.
c When the technique works, the woman often has twins or triplets. Explain why this happens.
d Draw a bar chart to show how the success rate for test tube fertilisation varies with a woman's age.

Key ideas

Now that you have completed this chapter, you should know:

- about external and internal fertilisation
- why some animals produce many more eggs and sperms than other animals
- how eggs and sperm are adapted for their functions
- the names and functions of the different parts of the human reproductive organs
- how and where fertilisation takes place in humans
- how the zygote divides to form an embryo and then a fetus
- how the placenta and amnion help to nourish and protect the fetus in the uterus
- what happens when a baby is born
- that inherited information is carried in the nucleus of the sperm and egg, and so is passed on to the child
- that humans care for their young much longer than any other animal
- how humans grow and develop to adulthood
- what menstruation is and why it happens.

Key words

adolescence	ovaries
amnion	oviduct
antibodies	ovulation
cervix	penis
cilia	period
development	placenta
embryo	pregnant
enzymes	puberty
external fertilisation	sex hormones
fertilisation	testes
fetus	umbilical cord
hormones	uterus
internal fertilisation	vagina
menstruation	zygote
milk	

End of chapter questions

1 The letters in these words are all jumbled up. Unjumble them, then copy each sentence and complete it using one of the words.

   oinnam   lkim   restuu   iangav   tcpaaenl

   a The _____ is the part of the mother's body where an embryo grows into a baby.

   b The _____ is an embryo's life-support system, which connects it to its mother.

   c The _____ is a bag around the embryo, which makes a fluid in which the embryo floats.

   d The baby is pushed out through the _____ when it is born.

   e A mother feeds her new-born baby on _____ .

2 Explain why fish and frogs produce so many more eggs than humans do.

3 Draw and label a diagram of a sperm cell.

4 Describe **three** changes that take place in a girl's body at adolescence.

5 The diagram shows the menstrual cycle of a woman.

   a Approximately how long does one menstrual cycle last?

   b At which point on the diagram is an egg released from the ovary?

   c Why does the lining of the uterus get thicker before the egg is released?

   d What happens to the lining of the uterus during menstruation?

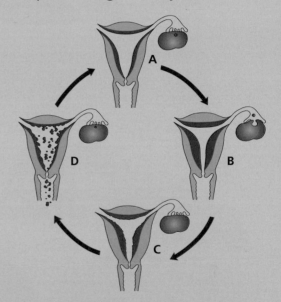

6 Discuss some the advantages and disadvantages of breast feeding rather than bottle feeding a young baby.

7 Most fish and amphibians use external fertilisation, but there are some exceptions to the rule. Find out about how one of these animals reproduces.

   cichlid fish   sticklebacks   guppies   midwife toads

8 When a baby is born before it is fully developed, it may be kept in an incubator for the first few weeks. Find out about how the incubator helps to keep the baby alive.

9 Imagine you have been asked by a local health authority to design a leaflet to be given to all pregnant women, explaining why they should not smoke while they are pregnant. Design one page of this leaflet. It could contain pictures, words or both.

I am full of energy!

Where does this athlete get his energy from?

Look at the pictures below. These show lots of different **fuels**. Fuels are **sources of energy**. They release energy when they are burned.

1 How many different types of fuel can you see being used? What are they being used for? Put the answers to these questions in a table similar to the one shown below. The first one has already been done for you.

Fuel	Use
Petrol	Move cars

Fuels contain **stored energy**. This energy is called **chemical potential energy**.

When we use energy it often changes into a *different* kind of energy.

What kinds of energy is the coal releasing as it burns?

Types of energy and their sources

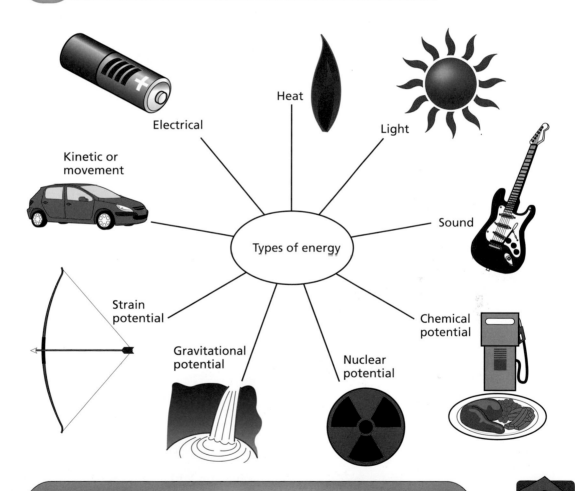

Electrical

Heat

Light

Kinetic or movement

Sound

Types of energy

Strain potential

Gravitational potential

Nuclear potential

Chemical potential

Try making up a *mnemonic* to help you remember the names of all the different types of energy. A mnemonic is a saying or sentence which contains the first letter of each of the words you are trying to remember. In this case your sentence should have nine words and their first letters should be h, l, s, c, n, g, s, k, and e. In this example the order of the words is not important.

Energy changes

When a candle burns, chemical potential energy is changed into heat and light.

When the toy is wound up and released, strain potential energy changes into kinetic energy and sound energy.

This loudspeaker is changing electrical energy into sound energy.

At the top of the waterfall the water has gravitational potential energy. As it falls its energy is changed into kinetic energy.

2 Look back at the diagram on page 66.
Write a sentence similar to the ones above to explain what energy change takes place when each fuel is burned.

The Bunsen burner

When we want to heat something in the science laboratory, we use a **Bunsen burner**.

The flame of a Bunsen burner can reach temperatures of over a 1000 °C. It is therefore important that you know how to use a Bunsen burner safely.

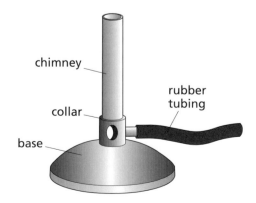

chimney

rubber tubing

collar

base

We can alter the temperature of a Bunsen flame by opening or closing the air hole. The flame is very hot with the air hole open and not so hot with the air hole closed.

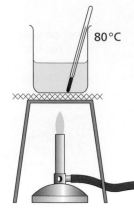

80 °C

60 °C

collar air hole open

collar air hole closed

The water is warmer with the air hole open because the Bunsen burner flame is much hotter.

3 Why is it important in the experiment shown above to have the same amount of water in each beaker?

4 a What fuel does a Bunsen burner use?

  b What is the energy change that is taking place?

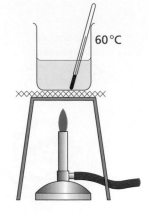

Fossil fuels

Coal, oil and natural gas are **fossil fuels**.

Plants and animals die.

How did these fuels form?

Fossil fuels are formed from the dead bodies of plants and animals.

Normally when plants and animals die they slowly rot away.

Sometimes, however, things happen to prevent them from rotting. If, for example, the bodies of dead plants and animals are covered with mud, no oxygen can reach them and without oxygen they will not rot. Instead they become preserved or **fossilised**. (Water is also needed for a dead plant or animal to rot.)

Over millions of years layers of rock slowly build on top of these fossilised remains. The high temperatures and pressures created by these rocks change the fossilised plants into coal and the tiny sea plants and animals into oil and natural gas.

They become covered with layers of mud. Over millions of years, rocks form on the dead remains.

Dead plants are eventually turned into coal.

5 a How long ago did fossil fuels start to form?
  b What normally happens when a plant or animal dies?
  c Name one thing that has to be present for a plant or animal to rot.
  d What two things are needed to change fossilised remains into coal, oil and gas?
6 Find out how many things at home and at school are powered *directly* by fossil fuels.

Will fossil fuels last forever?

Britain is fortunate because at the moment it has a good supply of coal, oil and natural gas.

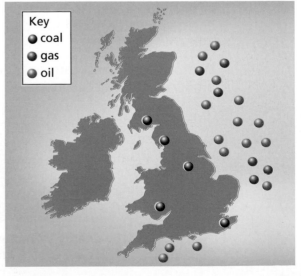

Key
● coal
● gas
● oil

However, fossil fuels will not last forever. Fossil fuels are **non-renewable**. They cannot be replaced once they have been used up because they take a very long time to form. Unfortunately we are using them up very quickly.

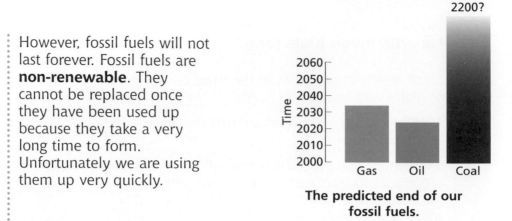

The predicted end of our fossil fuels.

7 a Which of these energy resources could run out in your lifetime?
  b How old will you be when these figures show we will run out of gas?
  c In what year do these figures show we will run out of oil?
  d Write a short story describing how your life would be affected if there were no fossil fuels.
8 Design a leaflet to explain to a Year 6 pupil what they could do to conserve energy resources.

Renewable energy resources

Fossil fuels are a very valuable source of energy. We must try to make them last as long as possible. One way in which we could do this is to use other sources of energy that can be replaced. These are called **renewable energy resources**.

Running water

Hydroelectric power stations change the gravitational potential energy of water stored in a dam into electrical energy.

Hydroelectric plants can produce cheap electricity. There are, however, often large costs to the environment. For example, plants and animals could lose their habitats due to flooding.

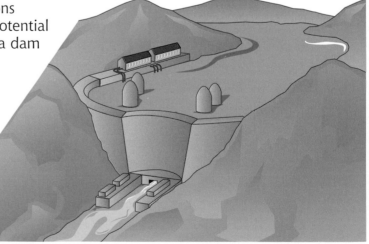

The energy stored by the water behind the dam is turned into electrical energy when the water is released.

9 a What energy transfer takes place in a hydroelectric power station?
  b How might the building of a hydroelectric power station affect the environment?

Wind

Wind turbines can harness the energy from the wind to produce electricity. They are very useful, particularly where homes are in remote areas.

However, if there is no wind, there is no energy. The building of lots of wind turbines might spoil the landscape and they can be very noisy.

 10 a Where are wind turbines most useful?
  b What are the disadvantages of wind energy?

Waves

Waves carry a lot of energy. If this energy could be harnessed, it would be a valuable resource.

A number of instruments have been produced which can generate electricity from wave energy. One of them is called Salter's Duck. It is made up of a chain of about 25 floats. As they bob up and down on the water, a pump is driven and electricity is generated.

However, large areas of these 'ducks' would be necessary to collect even a small amount of energy and storm damage could be a real problem.

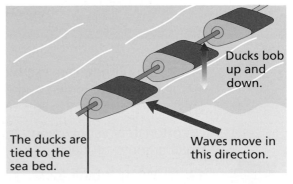

Ducks bob up and down.

The ducks are tied to the sea bed.

Waves move in this direction.

 11 a Why would wave energy only be useful in some countries?
  b What are the disadvantages of wave energy?

Hot rocks

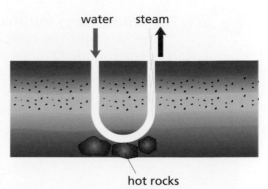

water   steam

hot rocks

Deep under the Earth's crust there are rocks that are very hot.

The heat is produced by nuclear reactions. Occasionally, where the Earth's crust is thin, these 'hot' rocks are found near the surface. Cold water can be pumped down to these rocks. It becomes heated and turns into steam.

Using geothermal energy is not a new idea. The Romans used this energy to provide central heating for their homes thousands of years ago.

Today, electricity generating plants are built near these areas and the steam is used to turn turbines which drive generators to produce electricity. Unfortunately, there are very few places where 'hot rocks' can be found close enough to the Earth's surface.

12 a Why are some rocks beneath the Earth's surface 'hot'?
   b How did the Romans use geothermal energy?
   c How can geothermal energy be used in power stations?

Biomass

Biomass is animal or plant material that is used to produce energy. Wood and animal dung are examples of biomass. They can be burned and the energy released used for cooking.

In some countries, cars use biomass fuels instead of petrol. Plants such as sugar beet are grown and then part of them is converted into alcohol. This is then used in the cars as a fuel.

Unfortunately very large quantities of plants are needed to make even a small amount of fuel.

13 a What is biomass?
   b Give some examples of how biomass is used as a source of energy.

Sunlight (solar)

Solar cells can change light energy from the Sun into electrical energy. They are very expensive to make, and will only work if it is sunny.

Solar panels collect heat energy from the Sun and use it to warm water. Again, this energy can only be collected if the Sun is shining.

YOU MAY BE ABLE TO DO WORKSHEET E5, 'INVESTIGATING SOLAR CELLS'.

Solar cells provide the energy needed by this telephone.

14 a Explain two ways in which solar energy can be used.
   b Why is solar energy a better source of energy in some countries than others?
15 Draw a diagram of different renewable energy resources. List the advantages and disadvantages of each of these energy resources.

Energy from the Sun

The diagrams below show that nearly all of our energy resources are formed from energy that originally came from the Sun.

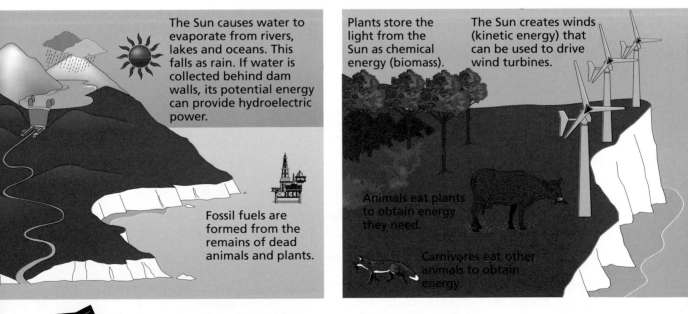

The Sun causes water to evaporate from rivers, lakes and oceans. This falls as rain. If water is collected behind dam walls, its potential energy can provide hydroelectric power.

Fossil fuels are formed from the remains of dead animals and plants.

Plants store the light from the Sun as chemical energy (biomass).

The Sun creates winds (kinetic energy) that can be used to drive wind turbines.

Animals eat plants to obtain energy they need.

Carnivores eat other animals to obtain energy.

16 Explain how the Sun's energy is used to create:
   a one renewable fuel
   b one fossil fuel.

How do we measure energy?

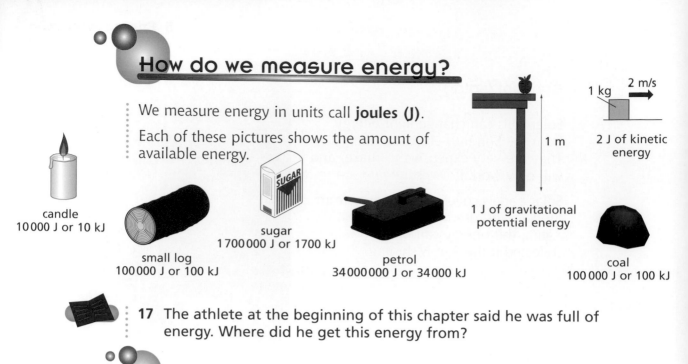

We measure energy in units call **joules (J)**.

Each of these pictures shows the amount of available energy.

candle
10 000 J or 10 kJ

small log
100 000 J or 100 kJ

sugar
1 700 000 J or 1700 kJ

petrol
34 000 000 J or 34 000 kJ

1 J of gravitational potential energy

2 J of kinetic energy

coal
100 000 J or 100 kJ

17 The athlete at the beginning of this chapter said he was full of energy. Where did he get this energy from?

Energy in foods

The food we eat provides us with energy. We need energy to keep us alive. Having energy allows us to do things.

Many food suppliers and manufacturers measure the energy in food in calories. 1 calorie is equal to about 4 kilojoules of energy. (1 kJ = 1000 J)

18 How could you find the amount of energy contained in the foods you have eaten today?

Many food packages have a panel which shows nutritional information.

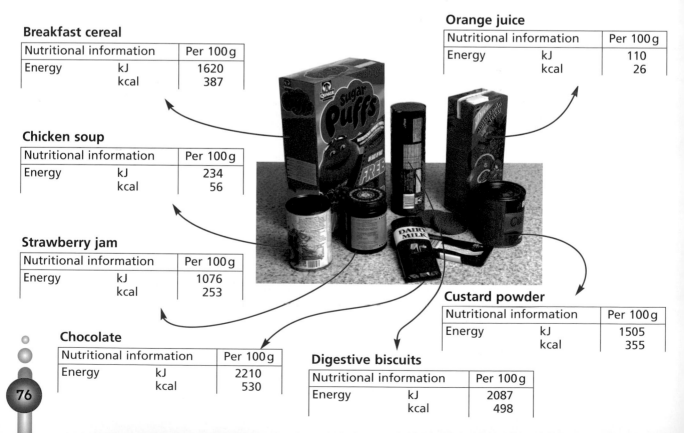

Breakfast cereal

Nutritional information		Per 100 g
Energy	kJ	1620
	kcal	387

Orange juice

Nutritional information		Per 100 g
Energy	kJ	110
	kcal	26

Chicken soup

Nutritional information		Per 100 g
Energy	kJ	234
	kcal	56

Strawberry jam

Nutritional information		Per 100 g
Energy	kJ	1076
	kcal	253

Custard powder

Nutritional information		Per 100 g
Energy	kJ	1505
	kcal	355

Chocolate

Nutritional information		Per 100 g
Energy	kJ	2210
	kcal	530

Digestive biscuits

Nutritional information		Per 100 g
Energy	kJ	2087
	kcal	498

19 a Why do all the foods show the amount of energy in 100 g of food?

b Which of the foods on page 76 contains the most energy per 100 g?

c If you ate 50 g of chocolate how much energy would you have consumed?

The table below shows the amount of energy in an average-sized portion of some different foods.

Food	Energy per serving (kJ)	Food	Energy per serving (kJ)
bread	320	crisps	550
cereal	800	chocolate	2200
pasta	500	fizzy drink	700
rice	500	apple	200
chips	1000	orange	200
boiled potatoes	400	peas	250
pizza	1250	carrots	80
cup of tea	100	baked beans	400
ice cream	400	beefburger	600

20 a How much energy is there in a meal consisting of a beefburger and a portion of chips?

b How much energy is there in a snack consisting of two slices of bread and a cup of tea?

c How much energy is there in a meal consisting of a pizza and an orange?

d Make up a typical breakfast, lunch and dinner from the table. Now work out the amount of energy contained in the foods you have chosen.

People with different lifestyles need different amounts of energy from their food. The table below shows some examples of these different energy needs.

	Approximate daily energy requirement
young child (8 years old)	8000 kJ
teenage girl	10 000 kJ
teenage boy	12 000 kJ
female office worker	10 000 kJ
male office worker	11 000 kJ
male manual worker	15 000 kJ

21 a How does the amount of energy you got from your made-up meals compare with the values shown in the table? If your list contained too much or too little energy what could you do to correct this?

b Explain why a teenage boy has a larger daily energy requirement than a male office worker.

c Draw a bar chart of the information in the table above.

John Tyndall was a famous physicist who was interested in energy.

He carefully calculated how much energy he would need to climb the Matterhorn mountain in the Alps. He worked out that all the energy he needed could be found in a ham sandwich – so that was all the food that he took with him for the journey!

Do you think that this was a sensible thing to do? Why?

The table below shows the results of a simple experiment to compare the amounts of energy contained in different types of food. A small amount of each type of food is burned and the heat energy released is used to warm a small boiling tube of water. The temperatures of the water before and after heating are noted so that the temperature rise can be calculated.

thermometer

stand

seeker

snack

Bunsen burner

mat

YOU MAY BE ABLE TO DO WORKSHEET E7, 'ENERGY FROM FOODS'.

Sample	Temperature at start (°C)	Temperature at end (°C)	Temperature rise (°C)
crisp	15	39	
snack	15	22	
cat biscuit	15	23	
cracker	15	90	
potato snack	15	36	

22 a Calculate the temperature rise for each of the different types of food in the table.

b Which food seemed to contain most energy?

c Suggest two things that must be done when carrying out this experiment to ensure it is a fair comparison.

Food chains

Plants make their own food using energy from the Sun. Grazing animals such as cows and sheep obtain their energy by eating plants. Most humans get their energy by eating meat from animals such as cows and sheep. This **transfer of energy** by eating is called a **food chain**.

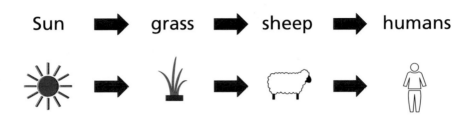

Sun ➡ grass ➡ sheep ➡ humans

Leaves get their energy from the Sun. Worms eat leaves. Voles eat worms. Owls eat voles.

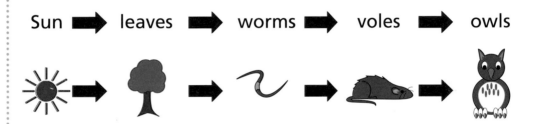

Sun ➡ leaves ➡ worms ➡ voles ➡ owls

In a food chain like this the leaves (or the trees on which they grow) are known as **producers** as they make their own food. Worms are known as **primary consumers**. Voles are known as **secondary consumers**. Owls are known as **tertiary consumers**.

In this pond the heron eats the fish which eat the pond plants.

Draw a food chain for the pond to show how the energy is passed on.

Draw a food chain to show how the energy is passed on.

23 a What does the fox eat?
b What does the rabbit eat?

Draw a food chain to show how the energy is passed on.

24 a What is the producer in this food chain?
b What is the primary consumer in this food chain?

James Joule

James Prescott Joule was a famous English scientist. He believed that scientists should carry out experiments to test out their ideas. Joule spent a lot of his time studying energy. He was particularly interested in energy transfer.

His enthusiasm for the subject was so great that even on his honeymoon he carried out some experiments. He was interested in the possibility that the temperatures of water at the top and at the bottom of a waterfall were different. His experiments confirmed that there was a difference. The water at the bottom of the waterfall was a little warmer.

Joule realised that this difference in temperature was due to an energy transfer. At the top of the waterfall the water is high up and so has gravitational potential energy. This potential energy changes into kinetic energy as it falls and the kinetic energy then changes into heat energy as it enters the pool at the bottom. This is why the temperature of the water was a little higher.

Joule had discovered what we now call the Law of Conservation of Energy. This says that the total energy before an energy transfer takes place is equal to the total energy after the transfer. It was a great discovery, and remains, even today, a very important idea in Science.

a Explain the meaning of the following words.
  i   enthusiasm
  ii possibility
  iii confirm
  iv gravitational potential energy
  v   conservation
b In what area was James Joule most interested?
c Describe in your own words one experiment that James Joule carried out. You may like to use other books or the internet to find out about his other experiments.
d Explain what energy changes took place in this experiment.
e What is James Joule's idea now called?

Key ideas

Now that you have completed this chapter, you should know that:

- coal, oil, natural gas and wood are fuels
- fuels are substances that are burned to release energy – normally in the form of heat
- coal, oil and natural gas are fossil fuels
- fossil fuels were formed from plants and animals that lived hundreds of millions of years ago
- fossil fuels are non-renewable sources of energy and should be conserved, where possible, for future generations
- wind, waves, running water, sunlight, biomass and geothermal are renewable energy resources
- energy is measured in units called joules (J)
- food provides the energy for living animals
- different foods provide different amounts of energy
- the initial source of energy in most food chains is the Sun.

Key words

Bunsen burner

chemical potential energy

energy transfer

food chain

fossil fuel

fuel

joule (J)

non-renewable energy resource

primary consumer

producer

renewable energy resource

secondary consumer

solar energy

source of energy

stored energy

tertiary consumer

1 Rearrange the following anagrams, then write out the word and its description.
   a gneyre   The ability to do work.
   b rruubbnnnees   Used in the laboratory to heat things.
   c lfue   Something which burns to release heat.
   d sambsoi   A renewable fuel.

2 Name the type of energy in each of these examples.

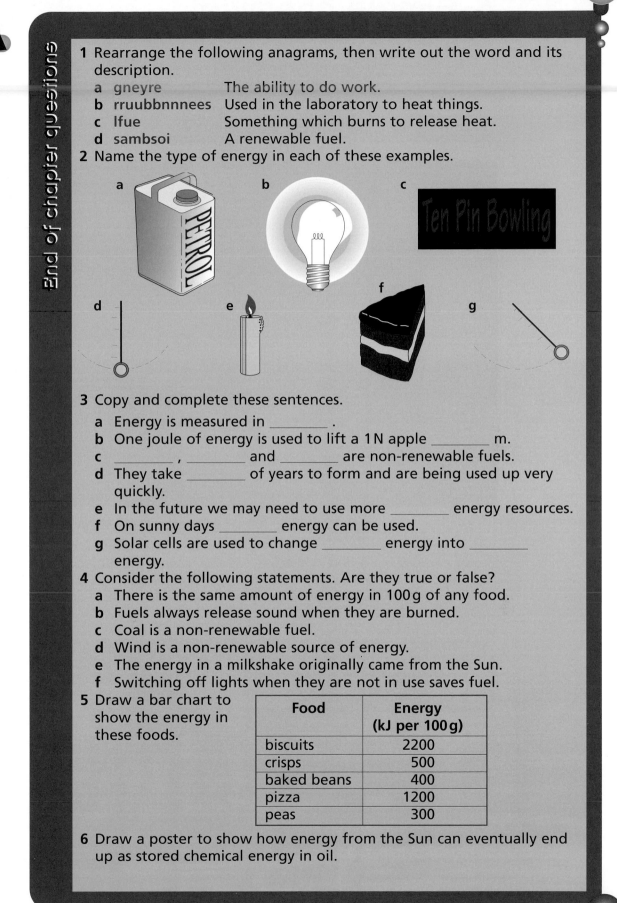

a PETROL b c Ten Pin Bowling

d e f g

3 Copy and complete these sentences.

   a Energy is measured in _____ .
   b One joule of energy is used to lift a 1 N apple _____ m.
   c _____ , _____ and _____ are non-renewable fuels.
   d They take _____ of years to form and are being used up very quickly.
   e In the future we may need to use more _____ energy resources.
   f On sunny days _____ energy can be used.
   g Solar cells are used to change _____ energy into _____ energy.

4 Consider the following statements. Are they true or false?
   a There is the same amount of energy in 100 g of any food.
   b Fuels always release sound when they are burned.
   c Coal is a non-renewable fuel.
   d Wind is a non-renewable source of energy.
   e The energy in a milkshake originally came from the Sun.
   f Switching off lights when they are not in use saves fuel.

5 Draw a bar chart to show the energy in these foods.

Food	Energy (kJ per 100 g)
biscuits	2200
crisps	500
baked beans	400
pizza	1200
peas	300

6 Draw a poster to show how energy from the Sun can eventually end up as stored chemical energy in oil.

6 Simple chemical reactions

What is a chemical reaction?

If you've ever watched a firework display, did you realise that you are watching lots of chemical reactions taking place? The different colours are produced by using different chemicals. Substances containing copper give blue colours, strontium gives red and magnesium gives a very bright white light. The colours are produced when these substances react with other substances in the firework.

> In a chemical reaction, one substance changes into another substance. The substance you end up with has different properties from the substance you started with.

YOU MAY BE ABLE TO DO WORKSHEET F1, 'HOW CAN YOU TELL WHEN A CHEMICAL REACTION IS HAPPENING?'

Most chemical reactions are not as violent or as spectacular as those that happen when fireworks go off! Many chemical reactions happen quite slowly and gently.

When a chemical reaction happens, the number of different substances you start with and end up with is not always the same. Sometimes, you might start with one substance and it changes into two or more different substances. At other times, you might start with two substances and they change into one.

Observing reactions

A good scientist observes things very carefully. 'Observing' means noticing what is going on. You can use most of your senses to give you clues that a chemical reaction is happening.

Seeing

If you see **bubbles** in a liquid, it means that a gas is being produced. The bubbles of gas work their way up to the top of the liquid and escape into the air. Your eyes may also be able to see **colours** changing, or a **flame** being produced. They may also notice that something is **disappearing**, or that something new is **appearing**. These all suggest that a chemical reaction is taking place.

Smelling

Sometimes, you can **smell** a new smell when a chemical reaction happens. This means that a new, smelly substance has been made. You must be very, very careful when smelling things – it might be something very unpleasant or dangerous.

Touching

Your fingers may feel that a test tube has got **warmer** or **colder**. Chemical reactions often release heat energy, making things hotter. Sometimes they use up energy, and make things colder.

Hearing

Sometimes, your ears can tell you that a reaction is happening. You might hear a fizzing or popping **noise**, or a whooshing sound. This usually means that a chemical reaction is happening very quickly.

1 Copy and complete this sentence, using some of these words.

acid   changes   explosive   neutralises   new   reaction

When a chemical _____ takes place, one substance _____ into a different substance. One or more _____ substances are formed.

2 Copy and complete this table to summarise how you can use your senses to tell that a chemical reaction is happening. Two observations have been written in for you, but there are more to be added.

Sense organs	Observations you can make
eyes	bubbles colour changes
ears	
nose	
temperature sensors in fingers	

Chemical reactions involving acids

Acids react with lots of different substances. You probably remember that alkalis can **neutralise** acids. This is an example of a chemical reaction. We start off with an acid and an alkali, and we end up with a liquid that doesn't contain either an acid or an alkali.

Acids also react with other substances, not only with alkalis. We are going to look at how acids react with metals and with carbonates.

How do acids react with metals?

YOU MAY BE ABLE TO DO WORKSHEET F2, 'REACTIONS BETWEEN ACIDS AND METALS'.

When a metal such as magnesium or zinc is added to an acid, bubbles appear. This tells us that there is a chemical reaction taking place.

The bubbles mean that a gas is being produced. The gas bubbles rise to the surface, and then the gas disappears into the air. The gas is colourless and invisible. It does not smell.

How can we find out what gas it is?

In fact, the gas is **hydrogen**. We can test it by holding a lighted splint where we think the gas is. If it *is* hydrogen, then we may hear a 'squeaky pop' noise.

How do acids react with carbonates?

YOU MAY BE ABLE TO DO WORKSHEET F3, 'REACTIONS BETWEEN ACIDS AND CARBONATES'.

There are many different kinds of carbonates. For example, some rocks are mostly made of carbonates. Limestone and marble are examples of carbonate rocks. Egg shells and snail shells are also made of carbonates.

When an acid is added to a carbonate, bubbles appear, so we know that a gas is being given off. The gas is colourless, so we can't see it – it just disappears into the air.

This gas is not hydrogen! If we hold a lighted splint in the gas, the splint goes out. There is no squeaky pop.

In fact, the gas is **carbon dioxide**. We can test it by bubbling some of the gas through a clear liquid called **lime water**. If the gas is carbon dioxide, then the lime water goes cloudy.

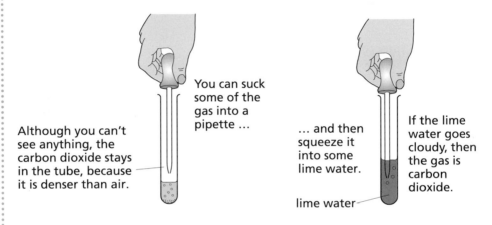

Although you can't see anything, the carbon dioxide stays in the tube, because it is denser than air.

You can suck some of the gas into a pipette ...

... and then squeeze it into some lime water.

lime water

If the lime water goes cloudy, then the gas is carbon dioxide.

3 Copy and complete this table.

Gas being tested for	What you do	What happens if the gas is present
hydrogen		
carbon dioxide		

4 Karen has found a bottle of a clear liquid. She thinks it might be an acid. She does not have any indicators or a pH meter, but she does have some egg shells.
What could she do to find out if the liquid is an acid?

Chemical reactions involving oxygen

Oxygen is all around us. It is in the air we breathe. Without it, no animals or plants could live.

Air contains a mixture of several different gases. All of them are colourless and none of them smell.

The gas which makes up most of the air is nitrogen. Oxygen is the next most common gas. The air also contains a little carbon dioxide. It does *not* contain hydrogen.

- nitrogen
- oxygen
- carbon dioxide
- rare gases

Burning metals in air

When something burns, a chemical reaction is taking place. The substance that is burning reacts with oxygen from the air.

When you burn magnesium in air, it burns with a bright, white flame. The reaction is quite fast and exciting!

The magnesium reacts with the oxygen in the air. The silvery-coloured magnesium metal changes into a white powder. The white powder is a new substance, formed when magnesium and oxygen react together. It is called **magnesium oxide**.

However, when you try to burn copper in air, not much seems to happen. The copper does not burn, so there is no flame. It does, though, gradually turn black. This black substance is produced when some of the copper reacts with oxygen in the air. It is called **copper oxide**.

From these two experiments we can see that the magnesium is more **reactive** than the copper.

Writing word equations

You can use a kind of shorthand to write down what happens during a chemical reaction. This shorthand is known as a **chemical equation**. If we use words in the equation, it is called a **word equation**. (Later on, you will find out how to write a different kind of chemical equation using chemical symbols instead of words.)

We have seen that when magnesium burns in air, the magnesium combines with oxygen and produces a new substance – magnesium oxide. Here is the word equation for this reaction:

$$\text{magnesium + oxygen} \rightarrow \text{magnesium oxide}$$

The substances to the left of the arrow are the ones that we start off with. They are the **reactants**.

The substances to the right of the arrow are the new ones that are produced in the reaction. They are the **products**.

5 What are the reactants when magnesium burns in air? What is the product?

6 a Write the word equation showing what happens when copper reacts with oxygen.
 b What are the reactants in this reaction? What is the product?

7 Pick out reactants and products from this list to write two different word equations summarising what happens when a metal burns in air. You can use the words once, more than once or not at all.

reactants	calcium	oxygen	lithium
products	hydrochloric acid	lithium oxide	hydrogen
	calcium oxide	carbon dioxide	

What is produced when fuels burn?

We have seen that when metals burn an oxide is produced. Does this happen when fuels burn?

You have already tried burning fuels in air in Chapter 5. We know that when a fuel burns, it combines with oxygen from the air. Your teacher may show you how to find out what is produced when a fuel called **kerosine** burns in air.

Kerosine is a **fossil fuel**. Fossil fuels contain carbon and hydrogen. When a fossil fuel burns, the carbon and the hydrogen each combine with oxygen from the air.

When the carbon in the fuel combines with oxygen, it forms an oxide of carbon called **carbon dioxide**.

When the hydrogen in the fuel combines with oxygen, it forms a hydrogen oxide. Dihydrogen oxide is such a common and important substance that it has a shorter name which we use all the time. It is **water**.

Pass the dihydrogen oxide, please!

8 The gas supplied to school laboratories is natural gas, which is known as **methane**. Methane is a fossil fuel. The apparatus below can be used to show what is produced when methane burns.

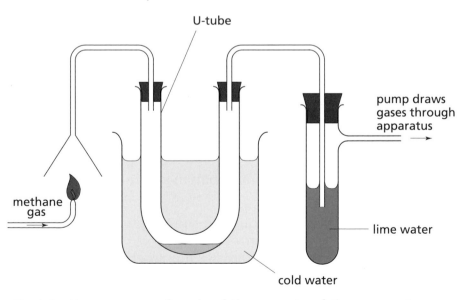

U-tube

pump draws gases through apparatus

methane gas

lime water

cold water

  a Explain the purpose of each of these parts of the apparatus.
     i the funnel **ii** the beaker of cold water **iii** the lime water
  b What would you see happening in the U-tube when the methane burns?
  c What would you see happening in the lime water when the methane burns?
  d Write the word equation showing what happens when methane burns in air.

Rock cake

Mel wanted to make a cake. He found a recipe for a sponge cake. The list of ingredients included margarine, flour, sugar, eggs and baking powder.

Mel looked in the kitchen cupboard, and found everything he needed. The carton of baking powder was almost empty, so he looked on the label to find out what it was. The label on the baking powder carton said 'contains tartaric acid and bicarbonate of soda'.

He said to himself, 'The recipe says it needs one teaspoon of baking powder. That is such a tiny amount that I'm sure it won't matter if I don't put any in the mixture'.

He mixed all the rest of the ingredients together, and spooned them into a cake tin. He put the tin into the oven and baked it exactly as the recipe said. It smelt really good.

When the cake had cooked and cooled down, Mel cut a slice for himself. It was horrible! The cake was solid and hard as a rock, not light and spongy as it should be.

a Bicarbonate of soda is a carbonate. Tartaric acid is an acid. When baking powder is mixed with water, it gives off a gas. Remembering what you have learnt about acids reacting with carbonates, what gas do you think this will be?

b Describe how you could test the gas that is given off when baking powder is mixed with water, to check your answer to part **a**.

c How do you think baking powder helps to make a light, spongy cake?

d Mel used a kind of flour called 'plain flour' when he made his cake. If he had used a different kind of flour, called 'self-raising flour', the cake might have been much nicer. Suggest what the flour manufacturers add to plain flour, to make self-raising flour.

Key ideas

Now that you have completed this chapter, you should know:

- that when a chemical reaction happens, new substances are produced
- what observations you can make that tell you a reaction is happening
- that hydrogen is produced when acids react with metals
- how to test a gas to find out if it is hydrogen
- that carbon dioxide is produced when acids react with carbonates
- how to test a gas to find out if it is carbon dioxide
- that when substances burn, they are reacting with oxygen
- what is produced when a metal burns in air, and when a fuel burns in air
- how to write a word equation.

Key words

appear	lime water
bubble	magnesium oxide
carbon dioxide	methane
chemical equation	neutralise
colder	noise
colour	product
copper oxide	reactant
disappear	reactive
flame	smell
fossil fuel	warmer
hydrogen	water
kerosine	word equation

1 Choose one of these words to match each description. You should use each word just once.

carbonate   carbon dioxide   hydrogen   oxide   oxygen

a This gas is produced when a metal reacts with an acid.

b When a substance burns, it reacts with this gas.

c This type of substance produces carbon dioxide when it reacts with an acid.

d You can test for this gas by holding a lighted splint in it. There will be a squeaky pop.

e This type of substance is produced when a metal burns in air.

2 The bubbles in a fizzy drink contain carbon dioxide. What could you do to prove the gas in the bubbles is carbon dioxide? What result would you expect?

3 There is something wrong with both of these word equations. Write each one out as it should be.

magnesium + oxygen = magnesium oxide
methane + air → water + carbon dioxide

4 Explain why magnesium burns more brightly and vigorously in oxygen than it does in air.

5 One kind of fire extinguisher contains carbon dioxide. When the fire extinguisher is set off, it sends a cloud of invisible carbon dioxide gas over the fire. The carbon dioxide forms an invisible 'blanket' covering the fire, keeping air away from it.
How does this put out the fire?

6 Make a poster to illustrate **one** of the chemical reactions you have learnt about in this chapter. You could include drawings of the reactants and products, and explain how you knew that a chemical reaction was happening.

7 The French chemist Antoine Lavoisier lived from 1743–1794. Before then, people thought that burning involved a substance called 'phlogiston'. Find out about Lavoisier, and how he disproved the phlogiston theory.

We cannot see forces but we can see their effects.

Look carefully at the diagrams below, then write two sentences for each. Write one sentence to describe how the force is being applied and a second to explain the effect of the force. The first one has been done for you.

A pulling force is being applied to the mule.
The force is making the mule move – just!

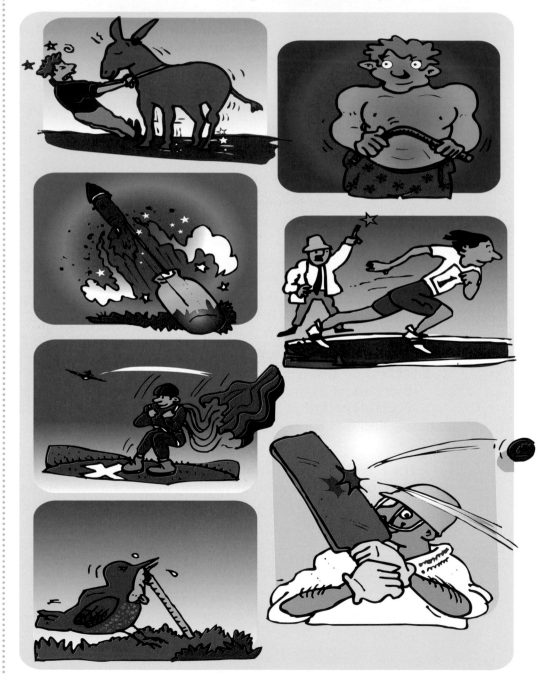

All forces are **pushes** or **pulls**.

Pushes and pulls can change the speed, direction or shape of an object.

> What do the forces in the three photographs below have in common?

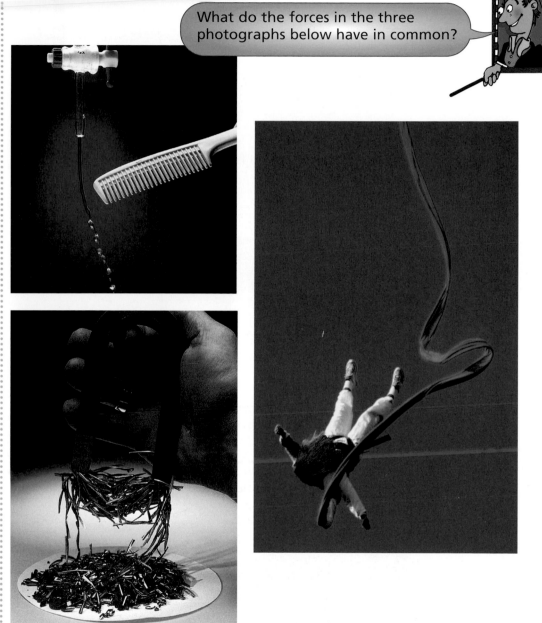

In each of these situations a pull force is being applied to an object without contact.

The water is being attracted to the charged comb by **electrostatic forces**.

The bungee jumper is being pulled downwards by a force we call **gravity**.

The iron strips are being pulled towards the magnet by **magnetic forces**. (The copper strips are not attracted by the magnet.)

Measuring forces

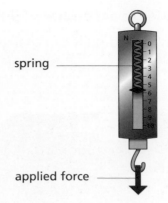

We measure the size of a force using a **newtonmeter**. A newtonmeter contains a spring. If a force is applied to the spring, it stretches. The larger the force we apply, the more the spring stretches.

spring

applied force

1 Look carefully at the two newtonmeters shown here.

Explain one way in which:

a the springs are different

b the scales are different.

We measure the size of a force in **newtons (N)**. If you hold an average sized apple in your hand you will feel a force due to gravity of about 1N. This force is the **weight** of the apple.

1N   ?N

YOU MAY BE ABLE TO DO WORKSHEET G1, 'MEASURING FORCES'.

Would your apple have the same weight on the Moon? Explain your answer.

2 Copy this table and fill in what you think are suitable values for those forces that have been left blank.

Activity	Size of applied force in newtons (N)
lifting one apple	1
opening a car door	10
pushing a car	100–200
squeezing toothpaste from a tube	
using a bicycle pump	
turning the page of a book	
lifting your school bag	
pressing the pedals on your bike	

Making your own newtonmeter

The diagram below shows the apparatus used by some pupils to make their own newtonmeter.

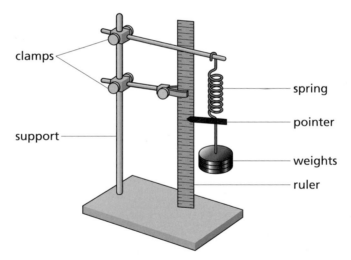

The pupils hung weights on the spring and then measured how much the spring extended. They recorded their results in this table.

Force applied to spring (N)	Extension of spring (mm)
0	0
1	3
4	12
6	18
8	24
10	30

3 a Copy these axes and draw a graph of the pupils' results.

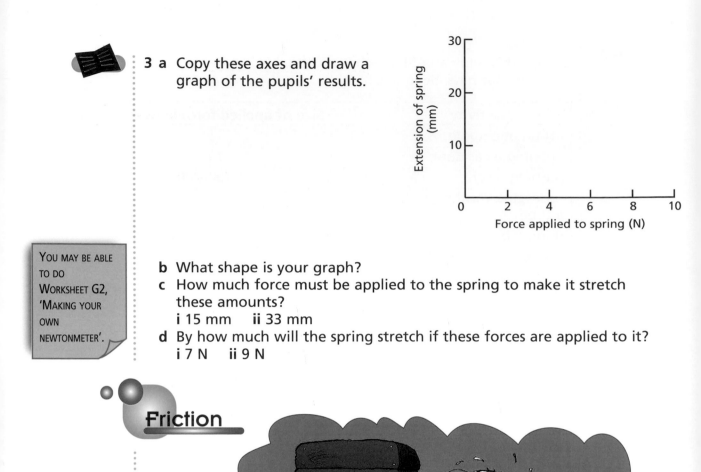

Extension of spring (mm)

Force applied to spring (N)

YOU MAY BE ABLE TO DO WORKSHEET G2, 'MAKING YOUR OWN NEWTONMETER'.

b What shape is your graph?
c How much force must be applied to the spring to make it stretch these amounts?
 i 15 mm **ii** 33 mm
d By how much will the spring stretch if these forces are applied to it?
 i 7 N **ii** 9 N

Friction

friction

pulling force

These workmen are applying a large force to the crate in order to move it. But there is a force trying to resist the movement. We call this force **friction**.

Friction is a force that opposes motion.

If the workmen can reduce the size of the frictional force it will make their job a lot easier. One way they could do this is to put the crate on rollers.

In what other ways could the workmen reduce friction?

Frictional forces are high if the surfaces where objects are in contact are rough.

friction

pulling force

Although a surface may look smooth to the naked eye, under the microscope we can see the roughness that causes friction.

Sometimes friction can be an advantage.

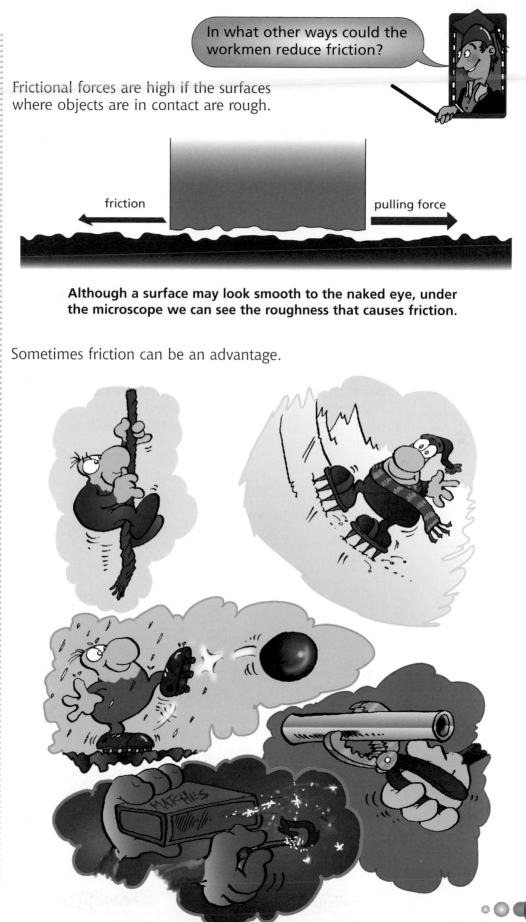

Sometimes friction can be a disadvantage.

4 a Suggest two ways in which we could increase the friction between two surfaces.
   b Suggest two ways in which we could decrease the friction between two surfaces.

YOU MAY BE ABLE TO DO WORKSHEET G4, 'FRICTION: TESTING DIFFERENT SURFACES'.

Really good slides have low frictional forces. This group of pupils has set up an experiment to test which of these slides has the lowest friction. What extra piece of apparatus do the pupils need?

5 Write a set of instructions the pupils should follow in order to find the best slide.

What steps should they take to make sure that this is a 'fair test'?

Can you predict which slide will have the lowest frictional forces? Give a reason for your choice.

If there is a lot of friction between two surfaces, they may become hot and wear away.

In this example the rise in temperature of the surfaces is used to light a fire.

You can use the friction between your hands to keep them warm.

YOU MAY BE ABLE TO DO WORKSHEET G5, 'FRICTION: TESTING BLOCKS OF DIFFERENT WEIGHTS'.

You can use friction to change the shape of one of the surfaces.

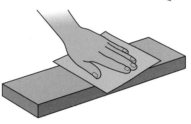

In this picture we want to try to avoid too much friction, so a liquid called a **lubricant** is added. The lubricant used here is oil. It forms a thin layer between the moving parts, stopping the chain and cogs from wearing each other away.

Cars need friction. It is very difficult to control this car, as there is very little friction between its tyres and the wet surface.

For a car to stop quickly there must be lots of friction between its tyres and the surface of the road. This means that:

• The tyres must have lots of tread – the amount of tyre touching the road.
• The road surface should be dry and rough.

The distance a car travels once the brakes have been applied is called the **braking distance**. If the tyres are worn, or the road is wet or icy, a car will need a longer braking distance.

The chart below shows us that the braking distance of a car also depends upon its speed.

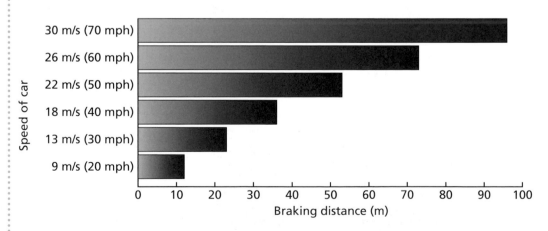

6 How far will a car travel after its brakes have been applied when it is moving at these speeds?
  a 18 m/s   **b** 30 m/s

We can see from this that the higher the speed of a car, the greater its braking distance.

This graph shows how the speed of a car changes when it is braking.

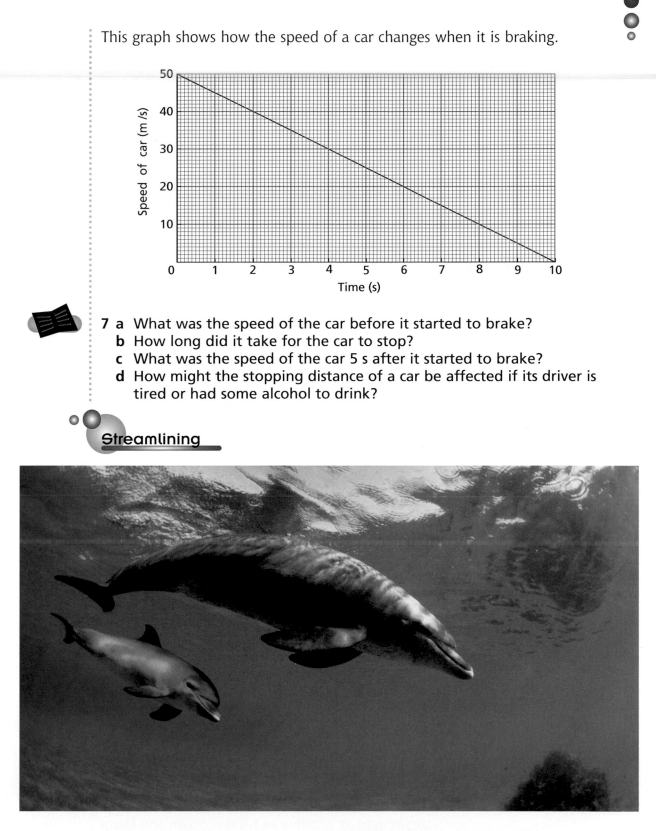

7 **a** What was the speed of the car before it started to brake?
   b How long did it take for the car to stop?
   c What was the speed of the car 5 s after it started to brake?
   d How might the stopping distance of a car be affected if its driver is tired or had some alcohol to drink?

Streamlining

As this dolphin swims there are frictional forces between it and the water. The faster the dolphin swims, the larger the friction. To keep these forces as small as possible, dolphins' bodies are shaped to cut smoothly through the water. They are **streamlined**.

These cyclists are experiencing frictional forces between them and the air. We call these forces **air resistance**.

How many different ways can you see that the cyclists have streamlined themselves and reduced air resistance?

Why, when we ride our bicycles, do we not need to be streamlined?

Name two places on our bicycles where we need friction.

YOU MAY BE ABLE TO DO WORKSHEET G7, 'STREAMLINING'.

Explain why this ski-jumper wants to be as streamlined as possible as he skis down the ramp.

How does he make himself streamlined?

When will the frictional forces be greatest?

Calculating speeds

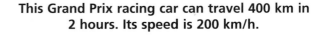

This sprinter can run 100 m in 10 s. His speed is 10 m/s.

This Grand Prix racing car can travel 400 km in 2 hours. Its speed is 200 km/h.

We can calculate the speed of an object by measuring how far it has travelled in a certain time, and then use the equation:

$$\text{Speed} = \frac{\text{distance}}{\text{time}}$$

Example 1
Calculate the speed of a dog that runs 50 m in 25 s.

$$\text{Speed} = \frac{\text{distance}}{\text{time}} = \frac{50 \text{ m}}{25 \text{ s}} = 2 \text{ m/s}$$

Example 2
Calculate the speed of a motorcyclist who travels 140 km in 2 hours.

$$\text{Speed} = \frac{\text{distance}}{\text{time}} = \frac{140 \text{ km}}{2 \text{ h}} = 70 \text{ km/h}$$

8 a Calculate the speed of a cyclist who travels 1000 m in 50 s.
   b Calculate the speed of a train that travels 600 km in 4 hours.

Balanced forces

In each of the diagrams shown below, forces are being applied to objects, but there is no change to the motion of the object.

In each situation more than one force is being applied. These forces are **balanced** so there is no overall force acting on the object.

The tug of war teams are pulling in opposite directions with the same force. These forces balance so there is no overall force and therefore no motion!

Gravity is trying to pull this man downwards but the branch of the tree is trying to pull him upwards. The forces are balanced so there is no motion.

This bottle is being pulled down by gravity. The table is pushing up with an equal force. We call this upward force the reaction. The forces are balanced so there is no motion.

9

I don't understand this. I am applying a forward force through my pedals but my motion is unchanged. My speed is not increasing.

Why isn't he increasing his speed? Suggest two ways in which he could increase his speed.

Where forces on an object are not balanced, there is an overall **resultant force** which causes the object to move in the direction of the force.

If you try to push a beachball under the water's surface, you will feel a force trying to push it upwards. This force is called an **upthrust**. An object floats because the upthrust acting on it from the liquid balances the object's downward force, which we call its weight.

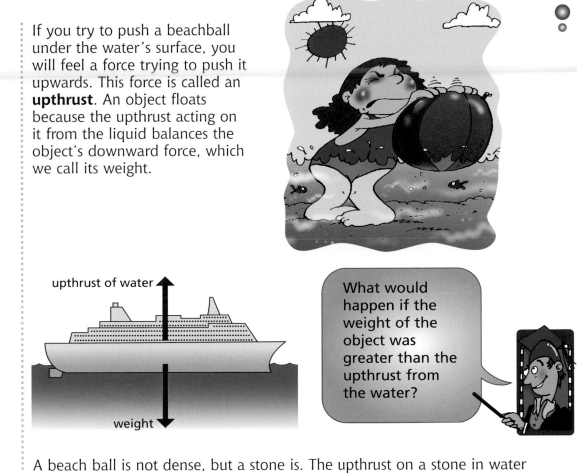

upthrust of water

weight

What would happen if the weight of the object was greater than the upthrust from the water?

A beach ball is not dense, but a stone is. The upthrust on a stone in water is not enough to make it float because its weight is greater than the upthrust. The forces are not balanced and the stone sinks.

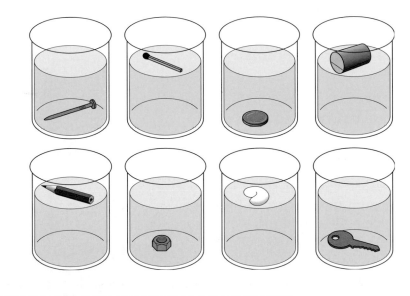

Is there a pattern that will allow you to predict if an object will float or sink in water?

Although this copper will not float on water, it will float on mercury. Upthrust is different in different liquids.

Is the upthrust from the water in the Dead Sea greater or smaller than the upthrust from the water in a swimming pool?

YOU MAY BE ABLE TO DO WORKSHEET G11, 'FLOATING AND SINKING'.

Mass and weight

This farmer has a real problem. He has gathered in his potato crop and now wants to record how well it has grown so that he can compare it with next year's crop. He could just count the number of potatoes. He realises that this would not be a good way of doing it as one year he may get lots of very small potatoes, and the next he might get fewer but much larger potatoes.

The solution to the farmer's problem is to put his crop onto some scales. The scales will measure the **mass** of his crop. The mass of an object tells us how much of it there is. We normally measure mass in grams (g) or kilograms (kg).

Once the farmer has measured the mass of his crop he will need to lift the potatoes so that he can take them away and store them. To lift the potatoes he needs to apply a force to overcome the force on the potatoes which is due to gravity and pulling them downwards. We call this force due to gravity, **weight**, and measure it in newtons (N).

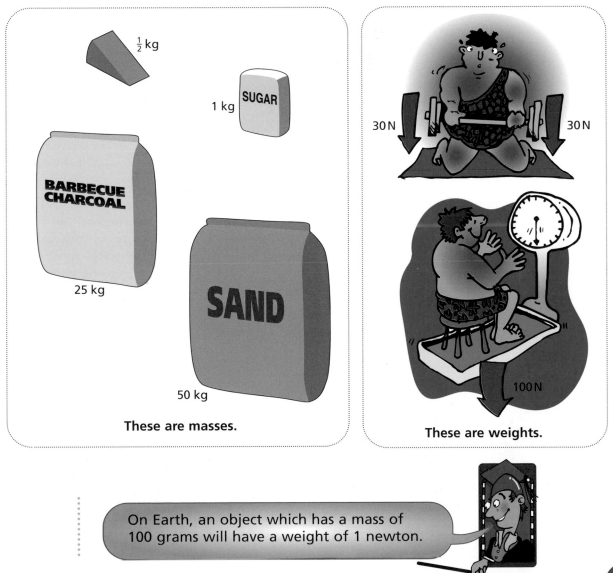

½ kg

1 kg SUGAR

BARBECUE CHARCOAL

25 kg

SAND

50 kg

These are masses.

30 N   30 N

100 N

These are weights.

On Earth, an object which has a mass of 100 grams will have a weight of 1 newton.

Sky diving

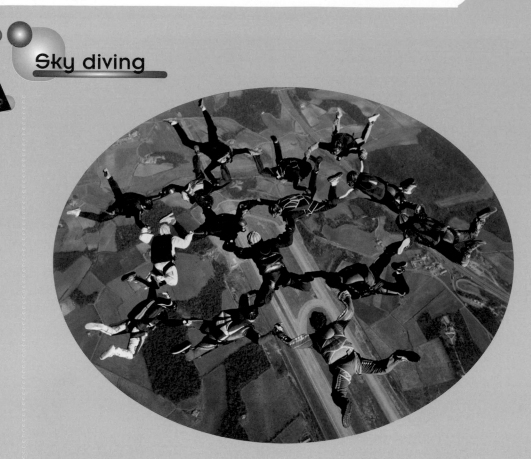

When an object falls, it is pulled downwards by the force of gravity. If the object is falling through the Earth's atmosphere, it will experience frictional forces called air resistance. The size of these forces depends upon the size, shape and speed of the object.

When a sky diver leaps from an aircraft he accelerates downwards. As his speed increases, so does his air resistance. Eventually, the force of air resistance and the force of gravity become equal and balanced. The sky diver now falls at a constant speed called his **terminal velocity**. At high altitudes, such as 3000 m, a sky diver's terminal velocity may be as high as 200 km/h. At lower altitudes, such as 1000 m, his terminal velocity is only about 150 km/h. These velocities are still far too high for the diver to survive a landing. His terminal velocity on landing should be approximately 15 km/h.

a What force pulls a falling object downwards?

b Explain in your own words the phrase 'air resistance'.

c Name three things that will affect the air resistance of a sky diver.

d Explain in your own words the phrase 'terminal velocity'.

e Why is the terminal velocity of a sky diver at 3000 m greater than that of the same sky diver at 1000 m?

f How does a sky diver reduce his terminal velocity before landing?

g Some sky divers jump from aircraft and then try to join together to make group shapes like the one shown above. Suggest how a sky diver is able to manoeuvre himself as he falls.

Key ideas

Now that you have completed this chapter, you should know:

- how to measure the size of a force
- that the size of a force is measured in newtons (N)
- that forces may affect the motion of an object
- that balanced forces will not affect the motion of an object
- why objects float
- that weight is caused by gravity
- the difference between mass and weight
- that friction is a force that opposes motion
- the effects of friction
- how friction can be increased or decreased
- what is meant by speed
- some factors that affect how quickly a car can stop.

Key words

air resistance	newtonmeter
balanced forces	push
braking distance	pull
distance	resultant force
electrostatic force	speed
friction	streamline
gravity	terminal velocity
lubricant	time
magnetic force	upthrust
mass	weight
newton (N)	

1 Rearrange the following anagrams, then write out the word and its description.
   a **orcfe**   A push or pull.
   b **nifcirot**   A force that opposes motion.
   c **edspe**   How fast an object is moving.
   d **sasm**   How much 'stuff'.
   e **dstlimanere**   A shape that reduces friction.
   f **suuttphr**   The force that keeps you afloat.
   g **iunlbctra**   This reduces friction between surfaces.

2 Draw a cartoon that shows one of the effects of applying a force to an object.

3 Name three types of forces that can be applied to an object without actually being in contact with the object.

4 Copy the four objects shown below and choose the correct stickers to show their weights and their masses.

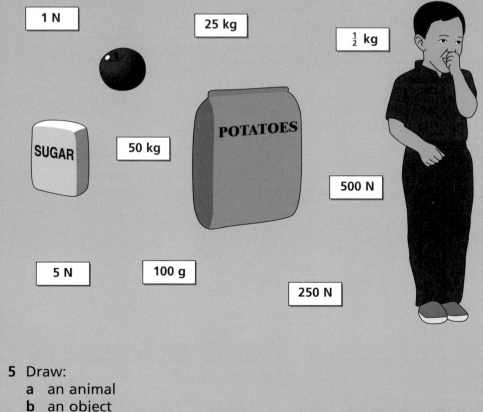

5 Draw:
   a an animal
   b an object
   which is streamlined so that it can move swiftly through water.

6 Draw:
 a an animal
 b an object
 which is streamlined so that it can move swiftly through the air.

7 This pupil weighed a piece of metal. It weighed 10 N. But when he weighed it in water, the metal only weighed 4 N.

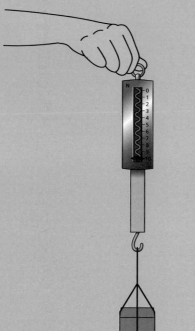

 Why did the piece of metal weigh less in the water?
 Do you think that the metal will float or sink in water? Explain your answer.

8 Name four things that will affect how quickly a car can stop.

9 Calculate the speeds of the following:
 a A cheetah that ran 150 m in 5 s.
 b A tortoise that moved 5 cm in 5 minutes.
 c A car that travelled 240 m in 6 s.
 d An aircraft that flew 3000 km in 2 hours.

10 Draw a concept map which includes balanced force, friction, upthrust, gravity, mass, movement and speed.

8 Environment and feeding relationships

How do habitats vary?

A **habitat** is a place where organisms live.

Can you name each of these habitats?

1 a Copy this table. Leave plenty of space underneath it, so you can add one more row later.

Habitat				
Some organisms which live there				

Write in the top row, the names of the four habitats shown on page 114. Then write the name of each of these organisms under their habitat.

Different habitats have different features. We call the features of the habitat that affect the animals and plants that live there **environmental factors**.

b Add a third row in your table, and give it the heading – Environmental factors. Then write each of these environmental factors underneath the habitat in which it is found.

    very hot days and very cold nights
    heavy rainfall
    high temperatures
    very dry air and soil
    big changes in the water level twice a day
    shortage of water
    little light reaches the bottom

Tip – some of them are found in more than one habitat!

Habitats in a pond

The four habitats in your table all cover very large areas. However, the environmental factors in a habitat are not usually the same throughout the whole habitat.

A pond is a habitat for many different animals and plants. The environmental factors are different in different parts of the pond.

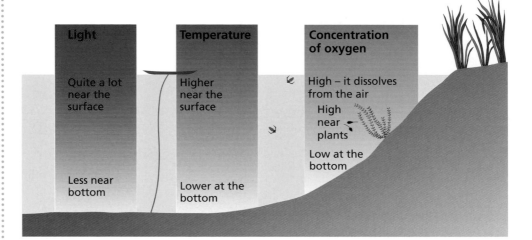

Sun

Light

Quite a lot near the surface

Less near bottom

Temperature

Higher near the surface

Lower at the bottom

Concentration of oxygen

High – it dissolves from the air

High near plants

Low at the bottom

2 Why can't pond weeds grow at the bottom of a deep pond?

Finding the best place

If you are a small animal, then perhaps only a small part of a habitat has environmental factors that are right for you. How do small animals find the best place for them to live?

Jovanka and Lubna turned over an old log that was lying near the school car park. There were lots of woodlice underneath the log. As soon as the log was turned over, the woodlice started scurrying about and hiding under the bark.

I wonder how they know what to do. Do they think, 'I must get underneath this bark and hide'?

I don't think that woodlice really think at all. Look what they are doing. Before we turned the log over, they must have been resting quietly. Now they are just running around all over the place. They don't really look as though they know where they are going. But as soon as they find themselves under the bark, they stop moving.

You may be able to do Worksheet H2, 'How does light affect the activity of woodlice?'

I wonder what makes them stop moving.

Maybe they stop moving when they are in the dark. Or perhaps when they are touching the bark. Or perhaps when the air feels damper to them.

How are organisms adapted to their habitat?

Each kind (species) of living organism is able to live in a particular habitat. Each has special features which help it to survive in that habitat. These special features are called **adaptations**. The adaptations help the organisms to cope with the environmental factors in their habitat. We say that each species is *adapted* to its habitat.

3 Look back at the table you drew for Question 1.

Copy each of these sentences below. Complete each sentence using the name of one or more of the animals from Question 1 in the first space, and the name of one of the habitats in the second space. The first one has been done for you.

> **Tip** – some sentences could apply to more than one habitat! If you find one like this, then copy the sentence out twice – once for one habitat, and then again for the second habitat.

a <u>Camels and gerbils</u> can live in a <u>desert</u> because they are able to survive with very little water to drink.

b _____ can live in _____ because they are able to breathe under water.

c _____ can live in _____ because they are able to burrow under the sand to escape the hottest part of the day.

d _____ can live in _____ because they are able to walk on the surface of water.

e _____ can live in _____ because they are able to swim well.

f _____ can live in _____ because they are able to stop their body drying out in the hot sun.

g _____ can live in _____ because they are able to move around easily amongst the trees.

> Which of these habitats do humans live in? How do we manage to survive in so many different habitats?

How do habitats vary with time?

YOU MAY BE ABLE TO DO WORKSHEET H4, 'MEASURING CHANGES IN ENVIRONMENTAL FACTORS'.

We have seen how the environmental factors can vary in different parts of a habitat. Environmental factors can also vary at different times of day, or at different times of the year.

Daily changes

> Think about how environmental factors change during one 24-hour period in Britain in summer. How does the light change? What happens to the temperature? You may be able to test your ideas by measuring the changes outside your school.

The same place can feel very different at different times of day. During the daytime, when the Sun is shining on our bit of the Earth, it is light and warm. During the night time, when the Sun is shining on a different part of the Earth and not on us, it is dark and colder.

Some animals are most active during the daytime. They are **diurnal**. Other animals are most active during the night. They are **nocturnal**.

4 a Make a list of diurnal animals, and another list of nocturnal animals. You could include some or all of these, plus any others that you can think of.

  tawny owl   fox   bat   squirrel   robin   slug   hedgehog

b How do the nocturnal animals in your list find their way around at night?

c Can you think of any advantages of being a nocturnal animal, rather than a diurnal animal?

Seasonal changes

In Britain, environmental factors change quite a lot during the year.

In summer, the days are long and the nights are are short. It is often quite warm during the daytime, and even at night it does not get very cold.

In winter, the days are short and the nights are long. Even when the Sun shines, it does not get really hot. It may get very cold, both in the daytime and at night. There may be frost and snow.

a At what time of the year do you think each of these photographs was taken?

b What changes can you see in these photographs?

c Can you suggest reasons for these changes?

In Britain, the winter can be a difficult time for animals and plants to survive. Here are some of the main problems for them:

• If temperatures drop below 0°C, then the water in their cells might freeze. This can kill the cells.

• If the ground is frozen, then plants may not be able to absorb water from the soil.

• If you are an animal that feeds on insects or other small invertebrates, then there may not be enough food for you in winter.

Some of the ways that animals and plants survive the winter include:

being dormant	being inactive for a long period of time – like a seed
hibernating	spending the winter in a deep sleep
migrating	travelling from one place to another at different times of year

6 Name at least one animal or plant which survives the winter by:

a being dormant

b hibernating

c migrating

Feeding relationships

Plants feed by making their own food, in a process called **photosynthesis**. Plants are **producers**, because they produce the food that all other living organisms need.

Animals feed by eating other living organisms. They are **consumers**. Animals which only eat plants are **herbivores**. Animals which only eat other animals are **carnivores**. Animals which eat both plants and animals are **omnivores**.

Carnivorous animals which catch and kill other animals for food are **predators**. The animals which they kill and eat are their **prey**. Predators have adaptations to help them to catch and kill their prey. In order to help them to escape from their predators, prey animals also have adaptations.

Food chains

As you are reading this, your brain cells are working hard. To do this, they need energy. All our cells get the energy that they need from the food which we eat. The energy in food is **chemical energy**.

In Chapter 5 you looked at how energy is passed from one living organism to another, along a **food chain**. In a food chain, the arrows show the direction in which energy is passing from one organism to another. Here is an example:

grass → mouse → owl

So how did the energy get into the grass? Grass, like all green plants, is a producer. Inside the cells of the grass leaves, chlorophyll absorbs energy from sunlight. The sunlight energy is used to make sugar and starch. The sunlight energy is changed into chemical energy in the sugar and starch.

We can show this in the food chain:

sunlight → grass → mouse → owl

7 When cells in an animal's body need energy, they change the chemical energy in food into the kind of energy that they need.

Name the kind of energy that the chemical energy in food is changed into when each of the following things happen.

> Think hard – sometimes there is more than one kind of energy involved!

  a The cells in your leg muscles contract as you walk.
  b You sing.
  c You climb up a rope.
  d Your heart beats.

8 Can you think of an animal that changes the chemical energy in its food into light energy?

Food webs

A food chain is a simple way of showing one pathway along which energy is passed from one organism to another. But things are not really this simple!

Here is a diagram showing many different food chains in a wood. You can see how all the food chains link up with one another. A diagram like this is called a **food web**.

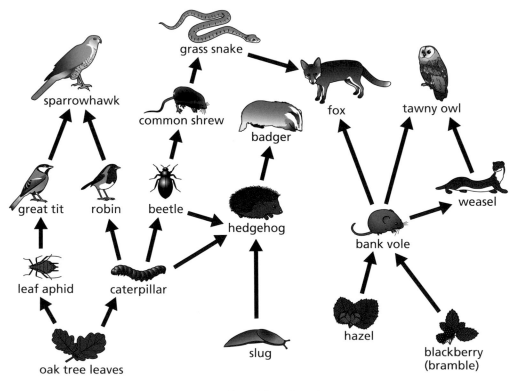

A woodland food web.

9 a Pick out three different food chains from the woodland food web, and write them down. (You don't need to draw the plants and animals unless you want to.)

b Underneath the name of each organism in your three food chains, write down whether it is a producer or a consumer. For each consumer, say whether it is a herbivore, a carnivore or an omnivore.

Competition

A food web shows that several different animals all eat the same food. For example, owls, foxes and weasels all eat bank voles.

In a good year, when the weather in spring and summer is warm and it rains enough to help the plants to grow well, the bank voles may have plenty of food and reproduce very successfully. There will be plenty of bank voles in the wood for all the predators to be able to find enough to eat.

But, in a bad year for bank voles when there is not much food for them, the bank vole population may be very small. There are not enough bank voles to feed all of the owls, foxes and weasels. We say that these predators are **competing** for the bank voles – their food. This does not mean that they get into arguments and battles about it! It just means that each of them has to work harder to get enough to eat. The more successful any predator is, the less food there is for the others.

10 Look back at the woodland food web.
Imagine that one year the bank vole population is almost wiped out by a very bad winter. For each of these animals, write one sentence explaining what you think might happen to the size of their population, and why you think that.

foxes   grass snakes

Try to include these words in your sentences:

predator   prey

Clues from old snails

Archaeologists dig into the ground to look for evidence of how people lived in the past. The deeper they dig, the older the remains.

An archaeologist investigated a burial mound, called a barrow, that was made about 5000 years ago. Today, the area around the barrow is treeless. The archaeologist wanted to know if it had always been like that. He had a theory that the land might have been covered by forest, long ago.

He dug carefully into the ground near to the barrow. He collected some snail shells from the soil. In the top layers, he found shells of a snail called *Vallonia*. Deeper down, he found shells of a different kind of snail, called *Discus*.

He looked in reference books to find information about these two kinds of snails. He discovered that, today, *Vallonia* is always found in places where the light intensity is high and the humidity is relatively low. *Discus* is always found where the light intensity is low and the humidity is high.

a Which snail shells were the older – *Vallonia* or *Discus*? Explain your answer.

b Would you expect the light intensity to be higher in a woodland, or in an open grassy area?

c In which of these two habitats would you expect humidity to be greater?

d Did the evidence which the archaeologist found support his theory? Explain your answer.

e Suggest what he should do to confirm his theory.

f Soil in some parts of Britain is acidic. Snail shells are made of calcium carbonate. Suggest why archaeologists do not find old snail shells in these acidic soils.

Key ideas

Now that you have completed this chapter, you should know:

• that a habitat is a place where organisms live, and that different habitats have different environmental factors

• that organisms have adaptations that help them to live in their habitat

• that the environmental factors in a habitat may vary in different parts of it, and also at different times of day or year

• that organisms may have adaptations to help them to cope with seasonal changes

• how to design a simple investigation into how environmental factors affect the activity of an animal, including thinking about sample size and controlling variables

• that predators and prey have adaptations to help them to catch prey or to avoid being caught

• how to draw food webs to show how different food chains link together

• that the arrows in a food web or food chain show the direction of energy transfer

• that food chains usually begin with a green plant

• that energy first enters a food chain in the form of light energy from the Sun

• how a rise or fall in the numbers of one organism in a food web might affect all of the others.

Key words

adaptation	habitat
carnivore	herbivore
chemical energy	hibernate
competition	migrate
consumer	nocturnal
diurnal	omnivore
dormant	photosynthesis
environmental factor	predator
food chain	prey
food web	producer

1 These words are jumbled up. Unjumble them, and then write each word followed by the definition which matches it.

ggtarimin   runotclan   bittaah   noitatdaap   batinenrghi

A The place where an animal or plant lives.
B A feature of an animal or plant which helps it to survive in its habitat.
C An animal that is active at night but not in the daytime.
D Spending the winter in a deep sleep.
E Travelling from one place to another at different times of year.

2 Gibbons live in the rainforest.

   a Describe **one** way, shown in the drawing, in which gibbons are adapted to live in the rainforest.

Monkey eagles eat young gibbons.

   b Describe **two** ways, shown in the drawing, in which monkey eagles are adapted to hunt and kill gibbons.

   c Copy and complete this sentence.
The monkey eagle is a p_____ and young gibbons are its p_____ .

End of chapter questions

3 a Write down a food chain with four organisms in it. Remember to begin the food chain with a plant, and to put arrows between the organisms.
b What do the arrows in your food chain mean?
c Name the producer in your food chain.
d Name a consumer in your food chain.
e Name a predator in your food chain.

4 Copy and complete this table, to show how some environmental factors are different in daytime and night time. In each box, write one of these words:

higher   lower   probably the same

Environmental factor	Daytime	Night time
temperature		
light intensity		
wind speed		

5 Seaweed grows on the rocks in a rock pool on the seashore. Limpets and periwinkles eat the seaweed. Seagulls and oystercatchers eat limpets and periwinkles.
a Draw a food web with all of these organisms in it.
b If all the seagulls move away, what might happen to the population of oystercatchers? Explain your answer.
c If all the seagulls and oystercatchers move away, what might happen to the population of limpets? Explain your answer.

6 Find out about plants and animals that live in one of these habitats:

a desert   a rainforest   the Arctic or Antarctic

Make a poster showing how the animals and plants in the habitat are linked together in a food web.

7 Books often say that every food chain starts with energy from the Sun, which is used by plants in photosynthesis. But that is not quite true! Find out about 'black smokers', which are found in the deepest parts of the oceans. Write a paragraph about them, and how the food chains around black smokers are different from food chains everywhere else on Earth.

9 Solutions

The Dead Sea is the saltiest sea in the world. Normal sea water contains about 40 grams of salt in every kilogram of water. But the water in the Dead Sea contains about 370 grams of salt per kilogram of water.

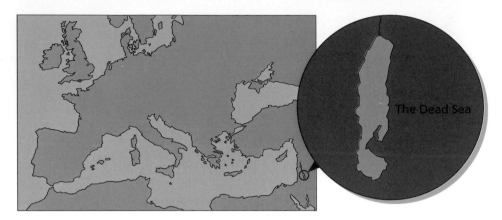

The Dead Sea

The water in the Dead Sea, like all sea water, is a salt solution. The salts are carried into the Dead Sea by rivers and springs. Rivers do not flow out of the Dead Sea, so all the salts that are brought into it stay there.

The climate near the Dead Sea is very hot and dry. The hot Sun evaporates some of the water from the sea. The water goes into the air as water vapour, and is carried off in the air to other places. But the salts do not evaporate. They stay in the Dead Sea. This has been happening over at least the past 10 000 years, which is why the Dead Sea is so very salty.

It is impossible to sink in the Dead Sea because the salts make the water denser than a person.

What is a solution?

All sea water, including the water in the Dead Sea, is a **solution**.
What exactly is a solution?

Mixtures

These pictures show some different liquids. All of them contain water.

| Sea water | Distilled water | Muddy water | Orange squash | Copper sulfate solution |

> Do all liquids contain water?

Distilled water is pure water. Pure water contains only one substance –
water. If we could see the tiny particles in some pure water, every particle
would be a water particle.

But all of the other liquids above contain something else as well as water.
They are all **mixtures**. If we could see the tiny particles in muddy water,
we would find not only water particles, but also particles of other
substances from the mud. If we could see the particles in sea water, we
would find salt particles as well as water particles.

Separating mixtures by filtration

YOU MAY BE ABLE
TO DO
WORKSHEET I1,
'FILTERING
MIXTURES'.

In some of the mixtures, the particles mixed in amongst the water particles
are quite big. If you look closely at some muddy water, you can probably
see the particles of mud. The mud particles are huge compared with the
tiny water particles.

If you pour muddy water through filter paper, some of the particles of mud are much too big to get through. They stay on the filter paper as the **residue**. The water goes through, and comes out looking much clearer. The water is called the **filtrate**.

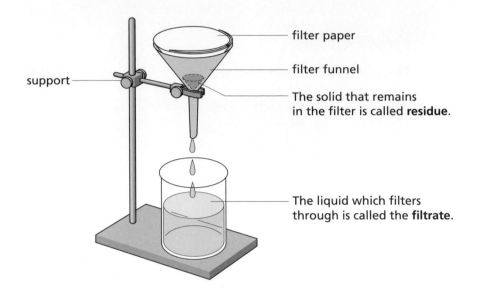

filter paper

filter funnel

support

The solid that remains in the filter is called **residue**.

The liquid which filters through is called the **filtrate**.

However, if you pour salty water through filter paper, *nothing* is left on the paper. The salt particles and the water particles all go through the paper. You cannot separate salt from water by filtration.

What happens when a solution is made?

When you add salt to water and stir it up, the salt seems to disappear completely. The water doesn't look any different with the salt in it than it did before you added the salt.

Where has the salt gone? We cannot see it, but it must be there. If you dipped your finger into the water and tasted it, you would be able to taste the salt.

When we mix the salt with the water, the salt breaks up into the smallest possible salt particles. Each tiny salt particle is separated from the other salt particles. Each of them is surrounded by water particles, and therefore we can't see them at all.

When this happens, we say that a **solution** has been made. In this example, the water is the **solvent**. The salt is called the **solute**. The solute **dissolves** in the solvent.

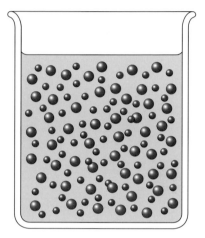

The particles in salt are packed closely together

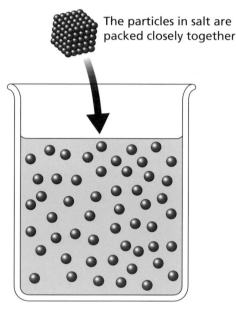

In liquid water, the particles are in constant motion and are randomly arranged.

When salt is added to water, the salt particles separate from each other and enter the spaces between the water particles.

How a solute dissolves in a solvent.

YOU MAY BE ABLE TO DO WORKSHEET 12, 'WHERE DOES THE SOLUTE GO?'

If you pour a solution through filter paper, all the different particles are tiny enough to go through. You can't separate the different substances in a solution by filtering.

1 Which of these statements about solutions are true?
   A All solutions are mixtures.
   B All solutions look clear.
   C Solutions are never coloured.
   D You can separate a solution by filtration.

2 Sally made a sugar solution by stirring some sugar into water.
   a What is the solvent in the sugar solution?
   b What is the solute?
   c Write a sentence or two explaining to Sally why the sugar disappears when it is mixed into the water. Use the word 'particles' in your explanation.

Separating solutes and solvents

Sometimes, we would like to be able to separate the water and solute from each other. You've seen that we can't do this by filtration. So how can it be done?

Separating the solute from a solution

In a salt solution, water is the solvent and salt is the solute. How could we separate the salt from the water in a salt solution?

On the shores of the Dead Sea, in Jordan, huge shallow lagoons have been made. Water from the Dead Sea is channelled into these lagoons. The hot Sun causes the liquid water in the lagoons to change into a gas. This is called **evaporation**. Only the water evaporates. The salts do not evaporate, and so are left behind. These salts include potassium chloride. Potassium chloride is used to make fertilisers, which are sold all over the world.

Water from the Dead Sea is held in large shallow lagoons. As some of the water evaporates, the water that is left behind cannot hold so much dissolved salt. So, the salt comes out of solution and forms deposits on the floor of the lagoon. Large machines scoop up and collect these salt deposits.

We can use a similar method to get salt from salty water. Rather than waiting for the Sun to make the water evaporate, we can heat it using a Bunsen burner. The water evaporates and the salt is left behind.

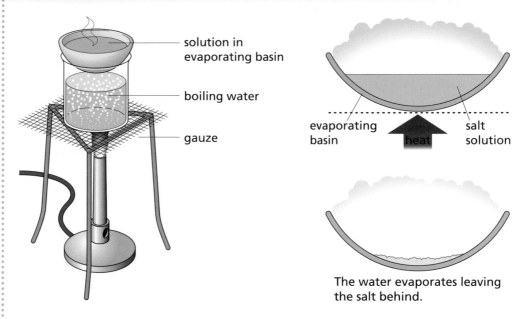

solution in evaporating basin

boiling water

gauze

evaporating basin

heat

salt solution

The water evaporates leaving the salt behind.

Evaporating a salt solution to dryness.

YOU MAY BE ABLE TO DO WORKSHEET 13, 'HOW MUCH SALT IS THERE IN ROCK SALT?'

3 Rock salt is – as you might have guessed – a rock made of salt. However, it isn't pure salt. There are lots of other things mixed up in it, such as mud.

Rock salt can be used to make salt for cooking. To make cooking salt, all the mud and other impurities in the rock salt have to be removed.

The salt in rock salt dissolves in water. The mud does not.
a How could you use filtration to get rid of the mud in some rock salt? Explain your answer.
b What could you do next to produce a sample of dry salt?

Separating the solvent from a solution

Sometimes it isn't the salt in salty water that we would like to use. Sometimes we would like to use the *water*! For example, some countries with hot, dry climates have very little fresh water available to them, but they may have plenty of sea water. How can we get pure water from salty water?

When water evaporates from salty water, the salts are all left behind. Only the water evaporates into the air. If we could catch this water and turn it back into liquid water again, we would have pure water.

The next diagram shows some apparatus which we can use to do exactly that. The process is called **distillation**.

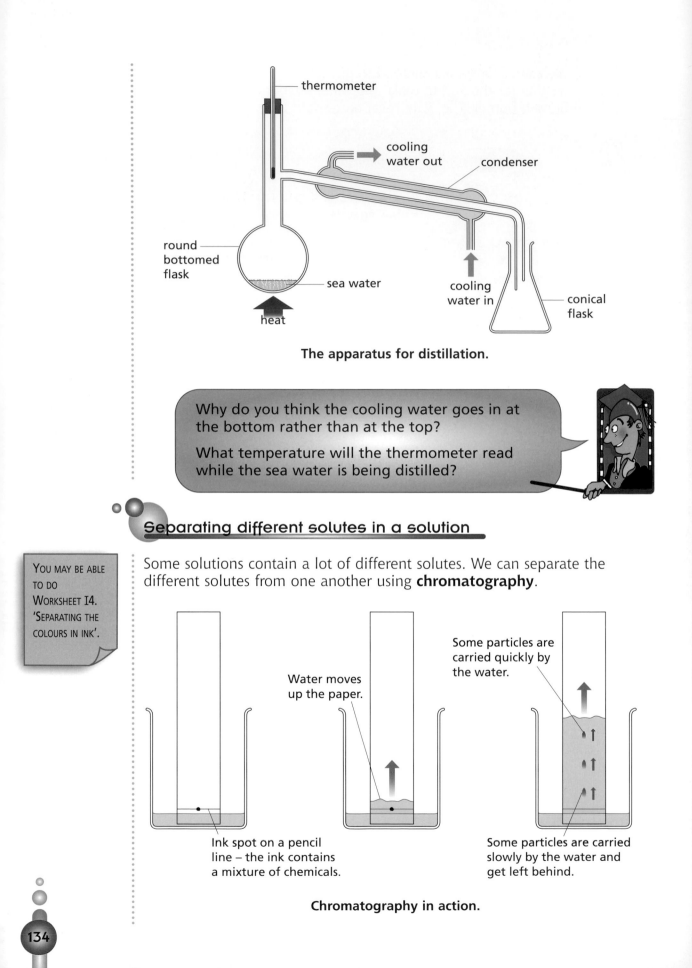

The apparatus for distillation.

Why do you think the cooling water goes in at the bottom rather than at the top?

What temperature will the thermometer read while the sea water is being distilled?

Separating different solutes in a solution

YOU MAY BE ABLE TO DO WORKSHEET 14. 'SEPARATING THE COLOURS IN INK'.

Some solutions contain a lot of different solutes. We can separate the different solutes from one another using **chromatography**.

Water moves up the paper.

Some particles are carried quickly by the water.

Ink spot on a pencil line – the ink contains a mixture of chemicals.

Some particles are carried slowly by the water and get left behind.

Chromatography in action.

What affects solubility?

If a substance dissolves in water, we say that it is **soluble** in water. If it does not dissolve, then it is **insoluble**.

4 Which of these substances are soluble in water? Which are insoluble in water?

sugar   chalk   salt   copper sulfate   mud

Saturated solutions

Joe likes his tea really sweet. He added sugar to a cup of tea and stirred it.

When he had drunk his tea, there was still sugar in the bottom of the cup. Some of the sugar had not dissolved.

Sugar is soluble in water, so why was there still some undissolved sugar at the bottom of Joe's cup of tea?

> YOU MAY BE ABLE TO DO WORKSHEET 17, 'HOW MUCH DISSOLVES'.

When sugar is added to water, the sugar breaks up into tiny particles. The tiny sugar particles spread out amongst the water particles. The sugar dissolves in the water, making a sugar solution.

But, if you keep on adding more and more sugar, eventually there is no more room between the water particles. The water has dissolved as much sugar as it can. The water is **saturated** with sugar.

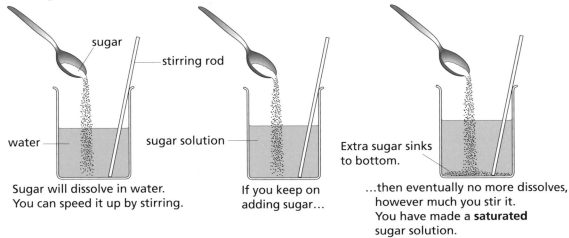

sugar

stirring rod

water

sugar solution

Extra sugar sinks to bottom.

Sugar will dissolve in water. You can speed it up by stirring.

If you keep on adding sugar…

…then eventually no more dissolves, however much you stir it. You have made a **saturated** sugar solution.

Making a saturated solution.

A solution like Joe's tea, which has absorbed as much solute as it possibly can, is called a **saturated solution**.

Solubility

Normally, more solute can dissolve in a hot solvent than in a cold one. If we try to dissolve copper sulfate in 100 g of water at 20 °C, we can only get about 20 g of copper sulfate to dissolve. If we heat the water up to 80 °C, then about 55 g of copper sulfate will dissolve.

So a saturated solution of copper sulfate at 80 °C contains more copper sulfate than a saturated solution of copper sulfate at 20 °C.

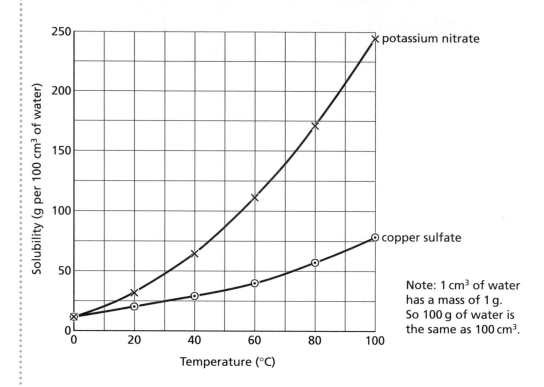

Note: 1 cm³ of water has a mass of 1 g. So 100 g of water is the same as 100 cm³.

5 a How many grams of copper sulfate will dissolve in 100 g of water at 60 °C?

b How many grams of copper sulfate will dissolve in 200 g of water at 60 °C?

c Alan said:
'According to the graph, potassium nitrate is three times more soluble than copper sulfate at 100 °C.'
Is Alan right? Explain your answer.

Crystallisation

Imagine you have made a saturated solution of copper sulfate in some very hot water. Because the water is hot, a lot of copper sulfate will dissolve.

Now imagine that the water cools down. As the water gets cooler, less copper sulfate can dissolve in it.

So what happens to the 'extra' copper sulfate as the water gets colder? The copper sulfate particles cannot fit in between the water particles any more. They begin to appear in the liquid. We can see crystals of copper sulfate forming. This is called **crystallisation**. You may remember making crystals in Chapter 1.

Copper sulfate solution.

Copper sulfate crystals.

If we heated the water up again, the copper sulfate would dissolve again. The crystals would disappear.

Dune beetles

The Namib desert, in southern Africa, is the oldest desert in the world. It is also one of the driest deserts. It hardly ever rains there.

The Namib desert lies on the west coast of Namibia, near to the sea. So there is plenty of water nearby, but there is no water for the animals in the desert to drink. Animals cannot survive by drinking sea water, because it is too salty. Sea water is a solution of many different substances dissolved in water.

Yet some animals are able to get drinking water from the sea. Winds blow from the west, over the sea and then over the Namib desert. As the air moves over the sea, water evaporates from the sea. The water is carried in the air as water vapour. The salt in the sea does not evaporate, so the water in the air is pure water without any salt in it.

On every dune near the sea, little black beetles live. At night, when it is cool, they climb to the top of their dune and stand with their heads down and their rear ends pointing upwards. As the wind gently blows over them, some of the water vapour in the air condenses on each beetle's body to form liquid water. The water slowly dribbles down the beetle's body, and forms little droplets next to its mouth – pure, fresh water in just the right place for the beetle to be able to drink it.

a Not many animals and plants can live in the Namib desert. Why do you think this is?

b Explain in your own words why the west winds blowing across the Namib desert contain water vapour.

c Explain in your own words why the water that condenses on the beetles' bodies does not contain any salt.

d Why do the beetles stand on top of the dunes to collect water, rather than lower down?

e Snakes live in the Namib desert. Snakes are carnivorous. Suggest where snakes get most of their water from.

Key ideas

Now that you have completed this chapter, you should know:

- that a mixture of an insoluble solid and a liquid can be separated by filtration
- that a solution is a mixture of a solvent and solute, which cannot be separated by filtration
- that a solution looks clear (but may be coloured)
- how to separate a solute from a solution by evaporating to dryness
- how to separate a solvent from a solution by distillation
- how to separate different solutes in a solution by chromatography
- that a saturated solution is one which cannot dissolve any more solute
- that many substances are more soluble in hot water than in cold water.

Key words

chromatography	mixture
crystallisation	residue
dissolve	saturated solution
distillation	soluble
evaporation	solute
filtrate	solution
filtration	solvent
insoluble	

1 Copy of each of these sentences, and complete them using these words.

    distillation   evaporation   filtrate   residue   solute
    solution   solvent

a When you filter a mixture of chalk and water, the chalk stays on the filter paper and is called the _____ . The water goes through the filter paper and is called the _____ .

b You can get pure water from salty water using _____ . You can get salt from salty water by _____ .

c Salt will dissolve in water to form a _____ . The salt is the _____ and the water is the _____ .

2 This is a list of processes which can be used for separating substances from mixtures.

    chromatography   distillation   evaporating to dryness
    filtration

Which process would you use for each of the following?

a Getting sugar from a sugar solution
b Finding out how many different coloured substances are present in green food colouring
c Getting sand from a mixture of sand and water
d Getting water from a mixture of sand and water
e Getting water from a copper sulfate solution

3 a Bomi wanted to find out how much ammonium sulfate would dissolve in 100 g of water. She added some ammonium sulfate to the water until no more would dissolve.
How would she know when no more would dissolve?

b What name is given to a solution in which no more solute can dissolve?

Bomi repeated this at ten different temperatures. Here is the graph that she drew to display her results.

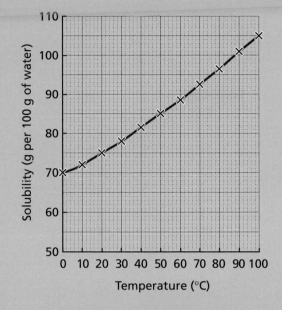

Solubility of ammonium sulfate.

c How much ammonium sulfate would dissolve in 100 g of water at 50 °C?

d If you wanted to dissolve 93 g of ammonium sulfate in 100 g of water, to what temperature would you need to heat the water?

4 Water is not the only liquid which can act as a solvent. Another example of a solvent is ethanol (alcohol). Many substances, such as grease, will not dissolve in water but *will* dissolve in ethanol.

a Explain why you cannot remove a greasy stain from your clothes using water, but you can remove it with ethanol.

b Sugar is soluble in ethanol, but salt is insoluble in ethanol. Sugar and salt are both soluble in water.

Paul has a mixture of salt and sugar. He also has some ethanol and some water. How could he:

i separate the salt from the mixture of salt and sugar

ii then get some dry sugar?

5 Make a poster to explain how to use **one** of the methods listed in question **2** to separate mixtures.

When Bill presses the switch, he knows that just one of his three bulbs will glow.

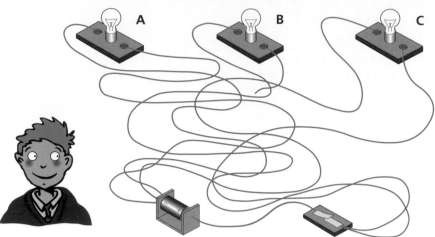

Can you work out which bulb will glow?

Can you explain why only this bulb glows?

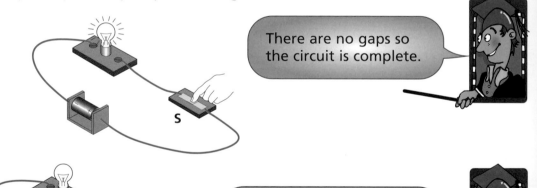

There are no gaps so the circuit is complete.

Now there is a gap so the circuit is incomplete.

You may be able to do Worksheets J1, 'Complete and incomplete circuits' and J2, 'Conductors and insulators'.

When the switch S is pressed, the circuit becomes **complete**. Electric **current** is able to travel around the circuit and the bulb glows.

When the switch is opened, the circuit becomes **incomplete**. Electric current can no longer travel all the way around the circuit and the bulb goes out.

1 a What is a complete circuit?
  b What is an incomplete circuit?

Conductors and insulators

Electric currents need something to travel through. They can travel easily through metals such as copper. Metals are good **conductors** of electricity. Electric currents cannot travel through plastics. They are **insulators**.

How could you use this circuit to test a material to see if it is a conductor or an insulator?

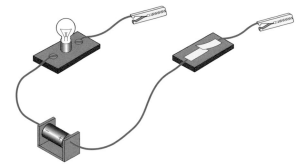

2 a What is an electrical conductor?
  b What is an insulator?
  c Write down five materials you think are good conductors of electricity.
  d Write down five materials you think are insulators.

Circuit diagrams

The 'bits and pieces' that make up a circuit, are called **components**. Most components are quite difficult to draw so we use easy-to-draw symbols instead.

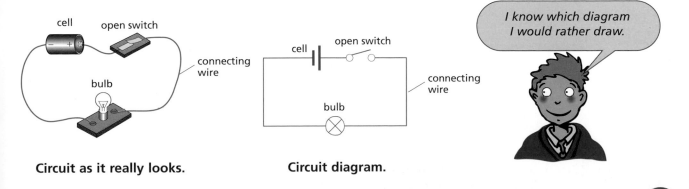

Circuit as it really looks.

Circuit diagram.

I know which diagram I would rather draw.

The table below shows some components and their symbols.

Component	Illustration	Symbol
cell		
battery		
switch		open switch closed switch
bulb		
connecting wire		

Using the information in the table above, draw the circuit diagrams for the following real circuits.

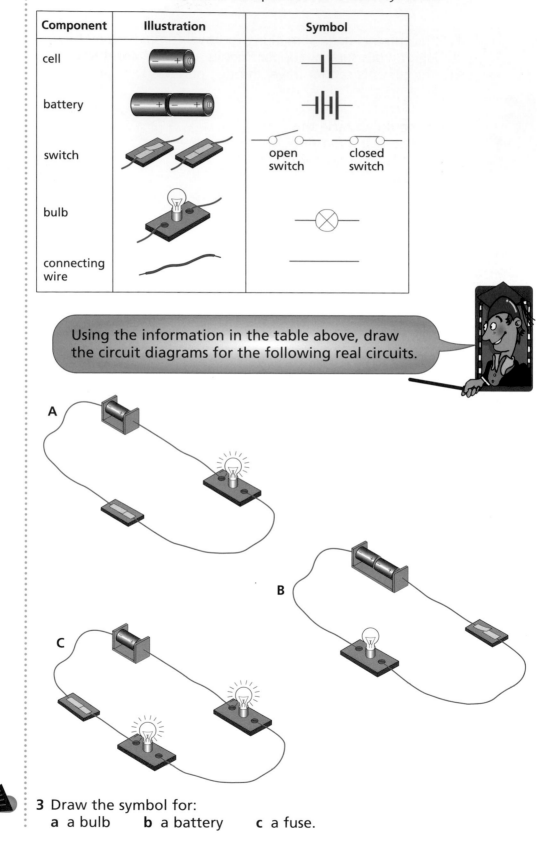

A

B

C

3 Draw the symbol for:
   a a bulb   b a battery   c a fuse.

electric
current

Cells and batteries

It is the **cell** in a circuit that makes the electric current travel around the circuit. A cell behaves as if it is an *electricity pump*.

The electric current is *pumped* from one side of the cell, all the way around the circuit and back into the other side of the cell.

If we want the bulb to glow more brightly we can create a stronger pump by connecting two or more cells together.

When two or more cells are connected together, they form a **battery**. You must take care to connect the cells so that they are pumping the electricity in the same direction.

> YOU MAY BE ABLE TO DO WORKSHEET J4, 'BATTERIES AND SWITCHES'.

These cells are connected together to form the battery for this radio.

4 In which of these circuits will the bulb glow brightest?

A   B   C   D

5 Copy and complete these sentences.
  a Cells behave as if they are electricity _____ .
  b They make the electricity move round the _____ .
  c If two or more cells are joined together, they form a _____ .

Measuring electric current

We measure the size of an electric current using an **ammeter** as shown in this photograph.

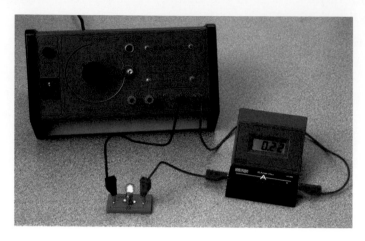

Electric current is measured in **amps (A)**.

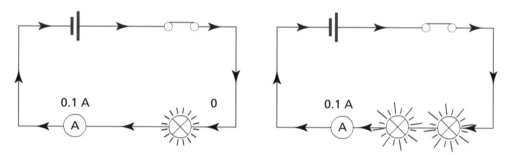

Measuring currents using an ammeter.

The table below shows the size of currents that might flow through different electrical appliances.

Appliance	Typical current
powerful electric fire	12 A
washing machine	10 A
hair drier	3 A
colour television	3 A
stereo system	1 A
bedroom light	$\frac{1}{4}$ A

Try to find out the size of the electric current that flows in these devices:
• A computer
• An electric toaster
• An electric kettle
• An electric drill.

Fuses

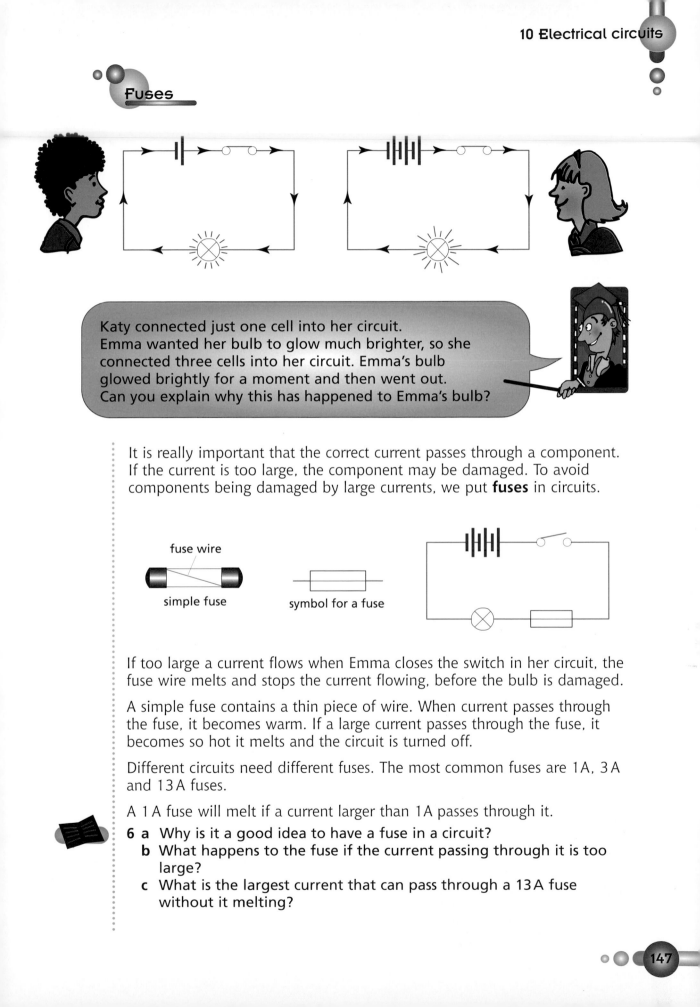

Katy connected just one cell into her circuit.
Emma wanted her bulb to glow much brighter, so she
connected three cells into her circuit. Emma's bulb
glowed brightly for a moment and then went out.
Can you explain why this has happened to Emma's bulb?

It is really important that the correct current passes through a component.
If the current is too large, the component may be damaged. To avoid
components being damaged by large currents, we put **fuses** in circuits.

fuse wire

simple fuse

symbol for a fuse

If too large a current flows when Emma closes the switch in her circuit, the
fuse wire melts and stops the current flowing, before the bulb is damaged.

A simple fuse contains a thin piece of wire. When current passes through
the fuse, it becomes warm. If a large current passes through the fuse, it
becomes so hot it melts and the circuit is turned off.

Different circuits need different fuses. The most common fuses are 1 A, 3 A
and 13 A fuses.

A 1 A fuse will melt if a current larger than 1 A passes through it.

6 a Why is it a good idea to have a fuse in a circuit?
  b What happens to the fuse if the current passing through it is too
     large?
  c What is the largest current that can pass through a 13 A fuse
     without it melting?

Series and parallel circuits

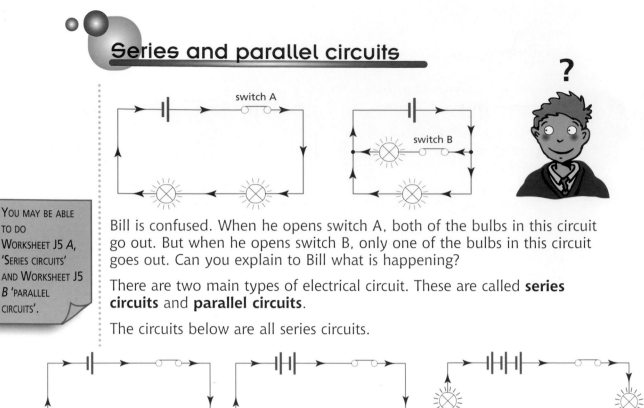

YOU MAY BE ABLE TO DO WORKSHEET J5 *A*, 'SERIES CIRCUITS' AND WORKSHEET J5 *B* 'PARALLEL CIRCUITS'.

Bill is confused. When he opens switch A, both of the bulbs in this circuit go out. But when he opens switch B, only one of the bulbs in this circuit goes out. Can you explain to Bill what is happening?

There are two main types of electrical circuit. These are called **series circuits** and **parallel circuits**.

The circuits below are all series circuits.

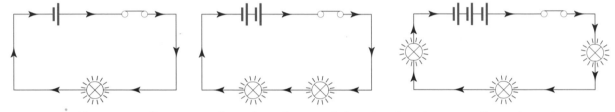

Place your finger on the wire of one of the circuits above. Follow the wire around the circuit. Now try this again with the other circuits.

You can see that in series circuits, there is only one path for the electric current to follow.

 7 Draw a circuit which contains a cell and three bulbs connected in series.

The circuits here are both parallel circuits.

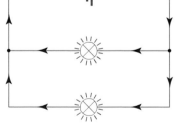

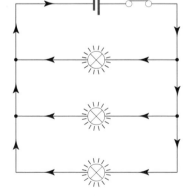

Again place your finger on the wire of one of the circuits and follow it round. Can you see the difference?

In parallel circuits, there are **junctions** and branches. When your finger arrives at a junction, there are several routes you can take. Currents in parallel circuits can travel along different paths.

8 Draw a circuit which contains a cell and three bulbs. The bulbs are connected in parallel.

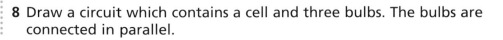

Turning currents on and off in series and parallel circuits

Look at this circuit diagram for a series circuit.

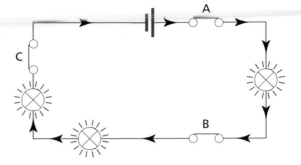

Starting with all the switches closed, explain what happens when:

- switch A is opened and closed
- switch B is opened and closed
- switch C is opened and closed.

Now look at this circuit diagram for a parallel circuit.

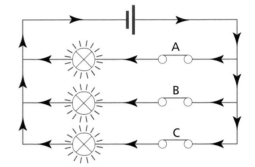

Starting with all the switches closed, explain what happens when:

- switch A is opened and closed
- switch B is opened and closed
- switch C is opened and closed.

YOU MAY BE ABLE TO DO WORKSHEET J7, 'MEASURING CURRENTS IN SERIES AND PARALLEL CIRCUITS'.

In series circuits, a switch will turn the whole circuit on or off. It is not possible to have just part of the circuit turned on.

In parallel circuits, it is possible to turn just part of the circuit on or off.

Can you decide which of these electrical appliances contain series circuits and which contain parallel circuits?
- Electric cooker
- Stereo systems
- Torch
- Three bar electric fire

9 Copy and complete these sentences.

a In _____ circuits there is only one path for the electricity to follow.

b If a switch in a series circuit is opened, the electric current _____ flowing, and all the bulbs go out.

c In a _____ circuit there are several paths the electric current can take. It is possible to turn just part of the _____ on or off.

Currents in series and parallel circuits

The current in a series circuit has the same value *everywhere*. The current leaving the cell is the same size as the current returning to the cell. Current is *not* used up as it travels around a circuit.

The currents in different parts of a parallel circuit may not be the same. But the current leaving a cell is still the same as the current returning to the cell. *Current is not used up.*

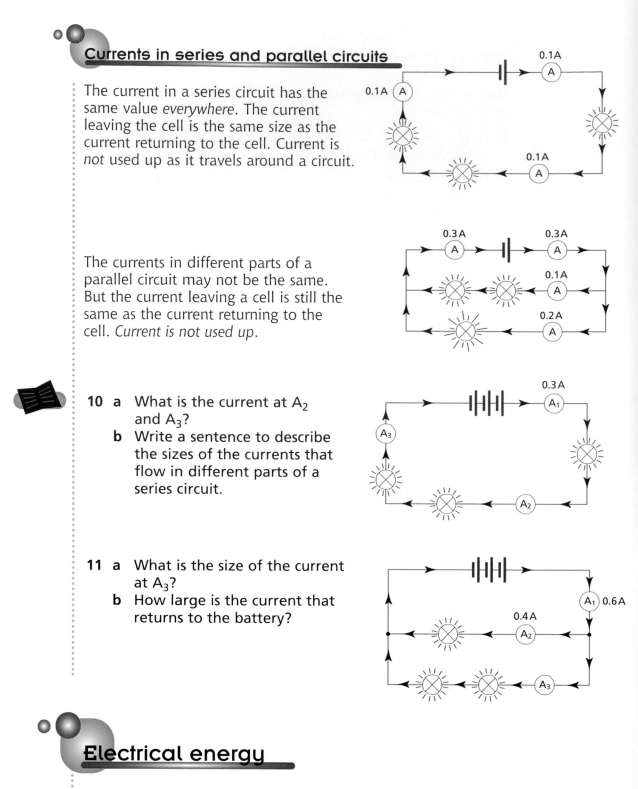

10 a What is the current at A_2 and A_3?

  b Write a sentence to describe the sizes of the currents that flow in different parts of a series circuit.

11 a What is the size of the current at A_3?

  b How large is the current that returns to the battery?

Electrical energy

When electricity passes through a cell or a battery it receives energy. Cells and batteries are sources of electrical energy.

Electric current carries this energy around the circuit to where it is needed. The current then returns to the cell or battery to 'pick up' more energy.

Circuit model

We can imagine that electric current picks up and delivers energy to different parts of a circuit in the same way as the train below receives and delivers its coal.

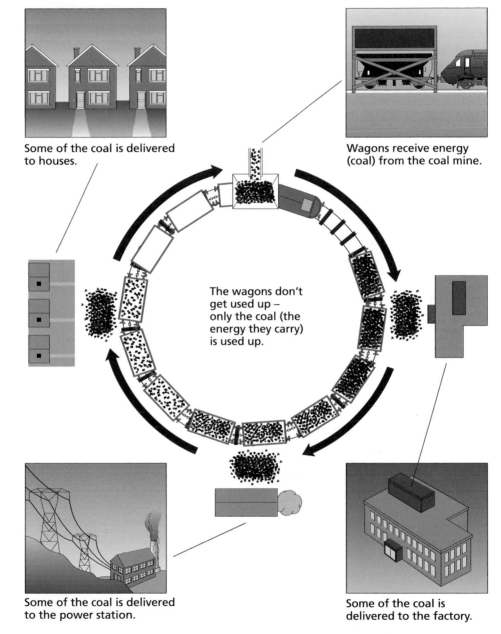

Some of the coal is delivered to houses.

Wagons receive energy (coal) from the coal mine.

The wagons don't get used up – only the coal (the energy they carry) is used up.

Some of the coal is delivered to the power station.

Some of the coal is delivered to the factory.

The wagons receive energy (coal) from the mine.

As they travel around the track, they give some of the coal:
- to the factory
- to the power station
- to the houses.

The wagons don't get used up – only the coal (the energy) they carry is used up.

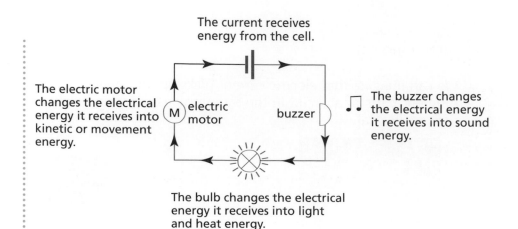

The current receives energy from the cell.

The electric motor changes the electrical energy it receives into kinetic or movement energy.

electric motor

buzzer

The buzzer changes the electrical energy it receives into sound energy.

The bulb changes the electrical energy it receives into light and heat energy.

In this circuit the current receives energy from the cell. As it travels around the circuit it gives some of this energy to the components to make them work, e.g.

- The buzzer changes the electrical energy it receives into sound energy.
- The bulb changes the electrical energy it receives into light and heat energy.
- The electric motor changes the electrical energy it receives into kinetic or movement energy.

The electric current does not get used up – it is the energy it is carrying that is used up.

Electrical resistance

All components in a circuit resist current passing through them.

Look at these two circuits.

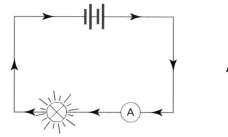

Circuit A

Circuit B

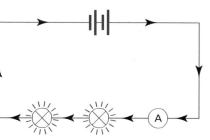

- Why is the bulb in circuit A glowing more brightly than either of the bulbs in circuit B?
- If you added a third bulb, in series with the two already in circuit B, how brightly would it glow? Explain your answer.

Current passes easily through connecting wires. We say that connecting wires have a **low resistance**.

Bulbs oppose the flow of current through them much more than connecting wires do. We say they have a **higher resistance**.

If we keep adding extra bulbs into the circuit like this, the resistance increases. The current flowing around the circuit will decrease and the bulbs will glow less brightly.

very, very, very small current

Adding extra bulbs like this makes no difference to their brightness.

YOU MAY BE ABLE TO DO WORKSHEET J8, 'RESISTORS'.

If bulbs are connected in parallel like those above they all glow with the same brightness as the same current passes through them.

This circuit contains a device called a variable resistor. It is used to alter the brightness of a bulb.

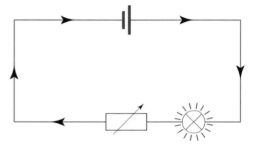

We can change the resistance of this component. It is called a *variable* resistor.

What happens to the brightness of the bulb when the resistance of the variable resistor is:
• increased   • decreased?
Suggest where a circuit like this might be very useful.

12 What does an electric current carry around a circuit?

13 Copy and complete these sentences.

   a All components _____ current passing through them.

   b Connecting _____ only resist the current flowing through them a little, so the electricity can pass through them quite easily. We say that they have a _____ resistance.

   c Connecting several bulbs into a series circuit will increase the _____ and therefore decrease the _____ .

   d If bulbs are connected in parallel they will have the same _____ .

Luigi Galvani

1_ La Grenouille de Galvani.

Luigi Galvani was a famous Italian scientist. As a young man, he became very interested in anatomy. He discovered how nerves carry messages around the bodies of animals and how they could be affected by electricity.

He noticed that the muscles in a frog's legs twitched and contracted during thunderstorms. He wondered if these movements could have been caused by atmospheric electricity.

To test his ideas, he tried touching the frogs legs with pieces of metal charged with static electricity. He found that the frogs legs did twitch and this confirmed his ideas.

a What nationality was Luigi Galvani?
b What does 'anatomy' mean?
c What do nerves do?
d What did Galvani notice happened during thunderstorms?
e How did Galvani test his ideas about what caused the frog's legs to twitch?

Key ideas

Now you have completed this chapter, you should know that:

- electricity can only flow if a circuit is complete
- cells and batteries are sources of electrical energy
- the components (parts) of a circuit can be represented using symbols
- there are two types of circuit – series and parallel
- in a series circuit, the more bulbs there are, the dimmer the bulbs will shine
- in a series circuit the current is always the same wherever it is measured
- when bulbs are connected in parallel, each bulb shines with equal brightness because the current is the same through each bulb
- fuses are safety devices which melt if too much current flows
- electric currents can effect the nerves in animals.

Key words

ammeter	fuse
amp (A)	incomplete circuit
battery	insulator
cell	junction
complete circuit	parallel circuit
component	resistance
conductor	series circuit
current	

1 Rearrange the following anagrams, then write out the word and its description.

a rerutnc   The flow of electricity.
b siteercans   Opposition to the flow of electricity.
c tyerbat   Two or more electrical cells.
d sefu   A safety device in an electrical circuit, which melts if too much current flows.

2 Name these components and draw their symbols.

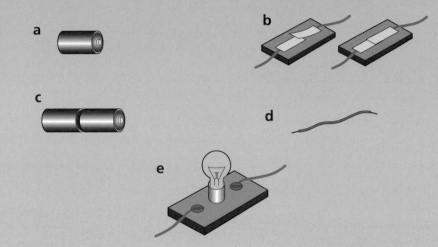

3 Consider the following statements – are they true or false?

a Electricity can only flow if a circuit is complete.
b Metals like copper are good insulators.
c In a series circuit, there is more than one pathway for the electricity to flow.
d The more bulbs placed in a series circuit the dimmer they become.
e In a parallel circuit there is a choice of pathway for the electricity.
f Fuses can be used to protect the components in a circuit.

4 Copy and complete these sentences.

a Electricity can only flow if a circuit is _____ .
b The more bulbs there are in a _____ circuit, the dimmer they become.
c The current at any point in a series circuit is always the _____ .
d In a _____ circuit the total current that flows is equal to the sum of the currents in the separate branches.
e If two identical bulbs are connected in parallel, their brightness is the _____ .
f The current is measured using an _____ .
g Cells are a source of _____energy.
h A number of cells joined together is called a _____ .

5 Consider the following circuits.
Why don't they work?
Redraw them so that they do!

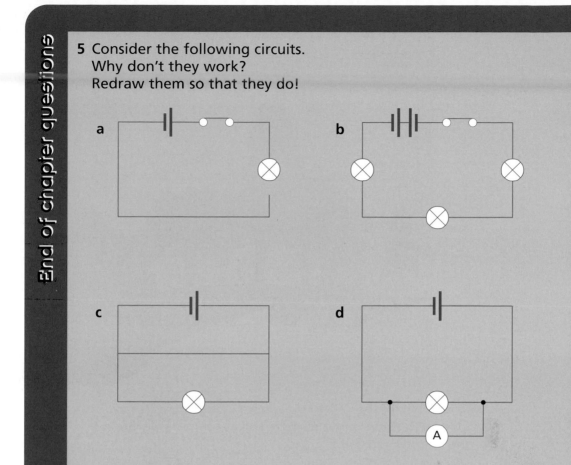

a

b

c

d

6 Find out how the lighting circuit on stairs works. This circuit allows you to turn the light on or off using the switch at the top of the stairs or the switch at the bottom of the stairs. Draw a circuit diagram to show how it works.

7 Draw a poster on electrical safety.

Alan's family had a new dog.
He took it out to show
to his friends.

He was quite upset when they laughed at him. 'Call that a dog?' they asked. 'It looks more like a cat!'.

1 Here are some different breeds of dogs.

a Make a list of at least five features that vary in the different dog breeds.

b What do all these dogs have in common that makes them different from cats?

Variation

Variation within a species

All domestic dogs belong to the same **species**, or group of living things. When we look at a dog, we (usually!) know that it is a dog straight away. Yet dogs are all different from one another. Even two dogs of the same breed can look very different.

We call these differences between living things, **variation**. No matter what species we look at, we can always find variation within it.

All human beings belong to the same species, but each of us is different from everyone else. Even identical twins are not absolutely the same in every way.

Are these twins identical?

YOU MAY BE ABLE TO DO WORKSHEETS K1, 'VARIATION WITHIN MY CLASS', AND K2, 'VARIATION IN LEAVES'.

What causes variation?

What is it that makes us all different from one another?

The differences between us are partly caused by our **genes**. We inherit our genes from our parents.

Genes are contained in the nucleus of each cell in our bodies. Every person gets half of their genes from their father, and half from their mother.

The mother's genes were inside the nucleus of the egg cell. The father's genes were inside the nucleus of the sperm cell. When the sperm fertilised the egg, their nuclei fused together. The new cell formed is called the zygote. Its nucleus contained a mixture of the father's genes and the mother's genes. Eventually, a baby was formed made up of hundreds of thousands of cells, each with all of these genes.

Another reason for the differences between us is our **environment**. This is all the things that happen to us during our lives, and the conditions in which we grow up and live. For example, a person who has a very poor diet when they are young may not grow as tall as someone who has plenty of good food to eat.

2 For each of these features of a person, say whether you think they are caused by:
  • genes only
  • environment only
  • both genes and environment

    height   eye colour   whether you are good at maths

3 A racehorse owner wants to have a horse that might win the Grand National. He decides to breed a foal, and then ask a trainer to train the horse so that it can run quickly over long distances, and jump large fences.
  a How should the racehorse owner choose the parents of the foal? Explain why this choice is important.
  b How might the horse's environment affect its chances of eventually winning the Grand National?

4 The leaves on the sunny side of a tree are often slightly larger than the leaves on the shade side. Is this variation caused by genes, the environment, or both? Explain why you think this.

Sorting living things into groups

Evidence from the past

Living things are all related to one another. Scientists think that, thousands of millions of years ago, the very first living things appeared on Earth. We don't know exactly how this happened, but we do know that they were very small. Each one was made up of just one cell.

Over long periods of time, some of these first organisms developed into other kinds. We know this because we find remains of them, called **fossils**, in old rocks. We can often find out how old the rocks are, so this can tell us how old the fossils are.

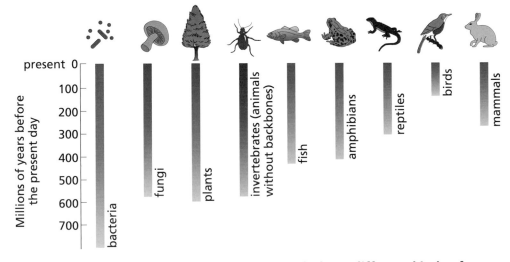

This chart shows how long ago we think these different kinds of organisms first appeared on Earth.

For example, in rocks that were formed in the Jurassic period, 150 million years ago, we find fossils of dinosaurs. Dinosaurs were reptiles. In slightly younger rocks, we find fossils of other reptiles, and of birds. These photographs show us how much the early bird fossils resemble those of dinosaurs.

Fossil of a dinosaur.

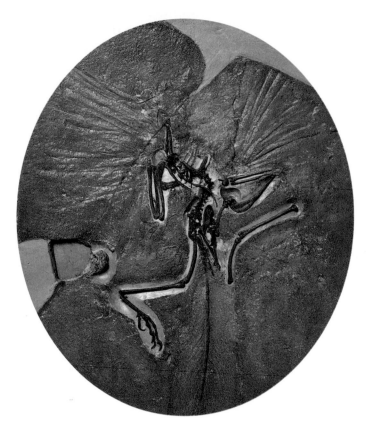

Fossil of a bird.

This evidence tells us that birds are closely related to reptiles. If we could trace the family history of a bird back for millions of years, we are pretty sure that we would find that its great, great (it would be at least 50 million greats!) grandfather was a dinosaur.

Even we are related to dinosaurs! And going even further back, we can find fossils of the animals that dinosaurs have developed from.

Going right back in time, to about 4000 million years ago, our distant ancestors were simple organisms, made of single cells, living in oceans and lakes.

Classifying living things

Biologists study living things. No-one really knows just how many different kinds of living things there are on Earth. About 1.4 million different species of organisms have been given names.

However, many people think that this is only a tiny proportion of living things that actually exist. There must be millions of species of bacteria in the soil, insects in rain forests and unknown creatures that live at the bottom of the deep oceans, that no-one has ever seen. Sometimes, new species of quite large animals are discovered even today. Some scientists estimate that we may have found only one tenth of all the species on Earth!

There are more different kinds of beetle on Earth than any other kind of animal.

To help study all of these different species of organisms, we put them into groups. This is called **classification**.

We classify living organisms according to how closely related we think they are. Species that seem to be very closely related go into the same group. Species that seem to be only distantly related go into different groups.

We are all related and are classified as *primates*.

5 Insects, birds and bats all have wings.

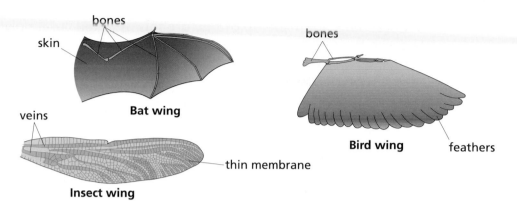

Bat wing

Bird wing

Insect wing

Explain how the structure of their wings shows:
   a that birds and bats are quite closely related to each other
   b that insects are not closely related to either birds or bats

Plants and animals

All the living organisms on Earth are classified into one of five big groups. These big groups are called **kingdoms**.

The two most familiar kingdoms are the **plant kingdom** and the **animal kingdom**.

A scuba diver found a blob of jelly growing on a rock in the sea. He tried to identify it from reference books, but could not find anything like it. He had a microscope, so he decided to start off by finding out whether it was a plant or an animal. How could he do this?

As well as the differences between their cells, we can see other differences between animals and plants. Perhaps the most important one is the way that they feed. Plants make their own food, using carbon dioxide gas from the air and water from the soil. Animals have to eat food that has been made by plants.

6 Explain why the way that plants feed makes them very important in food chains.

7 Coral reefs are made up of tiny organisms called coral polyps. Each polyp has a tiny ring of tentacles which it uses to trap food. The cells of the polyps do not have cell walls.
Are coral polyps animals or plants? Explain why you decided this.

Vertebrates and invertebrates

Animals can be classified into **vertebrates** and **invertebrates**. Vertebrates are animals with a backbone. Invertebrates are animals without a backbone.

8 Which of these animals are vertebrates, and which are invertebrates?

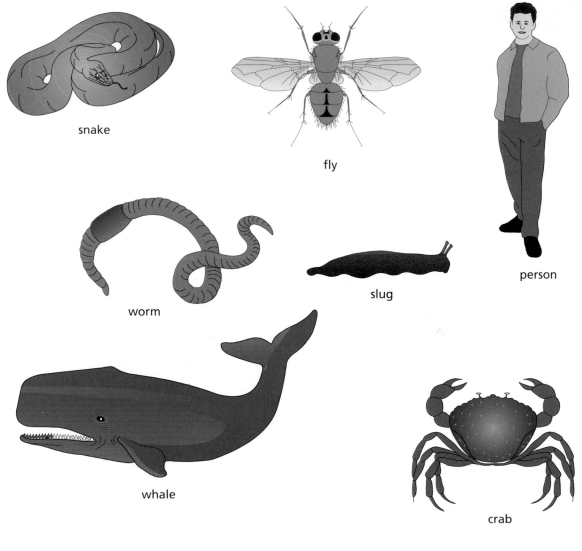

snake

fly

person

worm

slug

whale

crab

Classifying vertebrates

We classify vertebrates into five main groups. These are:

- **fish**

Fish have a body that is covered with scales. They have fins. They breathe using gills. They lay soft eggs in water.

- **amphibians**

Amphibians have a body covered with smooth, moist skin. They have four limbs (legs). They breathe using gills when they are young, and lungs when they are adults. They lay soft eggs in water.

- **reptiles**

Reptiles have a body covered with tough, hard scales. Most of them have four limbs. They breathe using lungs. They lay eggs with rubbery shells, on land.

- **birds**

Birds have a body covered with feathers. They have four limbs – two are legs, and the other two are wings. They breathe using lungs. They lay eggs with hard shells, on land.

- **mammals**

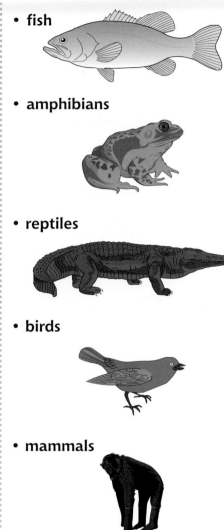

Mammals have a body covered with hair. They have four limbs. They breathe using lungs. Their young develop inside their bodies, so they do not lay eggs. They feed their young on milk.

9 Copy and complete this table to summarise the features of the five different groups of vertebrates.

Type of vertebrate	Fish	Amphibian	Reptile	Bird	Mammal
Skin covering	scales				
Limbs	no proper limbs – have fins				
Eggs	soft, laid in the water				
How they breathe	with gills				

The fieldmouse

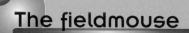

Read these two descriptions of a fieldmouse.

The Fieldmouse

Where the acorn tumbles down,
　Where the ash tree sheds its berry,
With your fur so soft and brown,
　With your eye so soft and merry,
Scarcely moving the long grass,
Fieldmouse, I can see you pass.

Little thing, in what dark den,
　Lie you all the winter sleeping?
Till warm weather comes again,
　Then once more I see you peeping
Round about the tall tree roots,
Nibbling at their fallen fruits.

Cecil Francis Alexander, 1815–1895

Yellow-necked field mouse

Identification: Body length 88–103 mm; tail length 92–134 mm; weight 22–48 g. Coat mostly brown, but often with a complete yellow collar or with a large yellow patch on the throat. Usually distinguishable from the wood mouse by the purer white and sharper edges of the markings on the underside. Tail with 170–240 rings.

Habitat: Woods.

Habits: Mainly nocturnal; emerges later than the wood mouse. Climbs and jumps very well. Lives under tree stumps, roots, and in crannies in rocks. Hides and stores food for the winter. Does not hibernate.

A Field Guide to the Mammals of Britain and Europe, Collins, 1977

a Which of these two descriptions gives you the better picture of the fieldmouse? Explain why.

b Suggest what each writer was trying to do when they wrote their descriptions. Have they both been successful?

c Suggest why the description in the *Field Guide* also refers to the wood mouse.

d Find one factual difference between the two descriptions.

e Choose any animal that you know well or can imagine. Write two different descriptions of it – first as a short poem that people will enjoy, and then a factual piece that would help them to identify the animal if they found one.

Key ideas

Now that you have completed this chapter, you should know:

- how to measure and record variation within a species
- that variation is caused by genes and by environment
- that all living things are related to one another
- that living things are classified by putting closely-related ones into the same group
- that animals and plants belong to different kingdoms
- that we can divide animals into invertebrates and vertebrates
- that vertebrates are classified into fish, amphibians, reptiles, birds and mammals
- how to decide which of these groups a vertebrate belongs to.

Key words

animal kingdom	kingdom
classification	plant kingdom
environment	primate
fossil	species
gene	variation
invertebrate	vertebrate

1 Copy the sentences, using words from this list to fill in the spaces. You can use each word once, more than once or not at all.

backbone   classification   evolution   fishes   heart
invertebrates   kingdoms   mammals   membranes
packed   related   vertebrates   walls

a Sorting living things into groups is called _____ . Scientists put closely _____ living organisms into the same group.

b Plants and animals are put into two large groups called _____ .

c All plant cells have cell _____ , but animal cells never have these.

d Animals can be divided into _____ and _____ , depending on whether or not they have a _____ .

2 The drawings show three horses.

a Describe two ways in which the two Shetland ponies differ from the Shire horse.

b Describe one way in which the two Shetland ponies differ from each other.

c For each of the three differences you have described, say whether you think the difference is caused by genes or by the environment.

3 This diagram summarises how animals are classified.

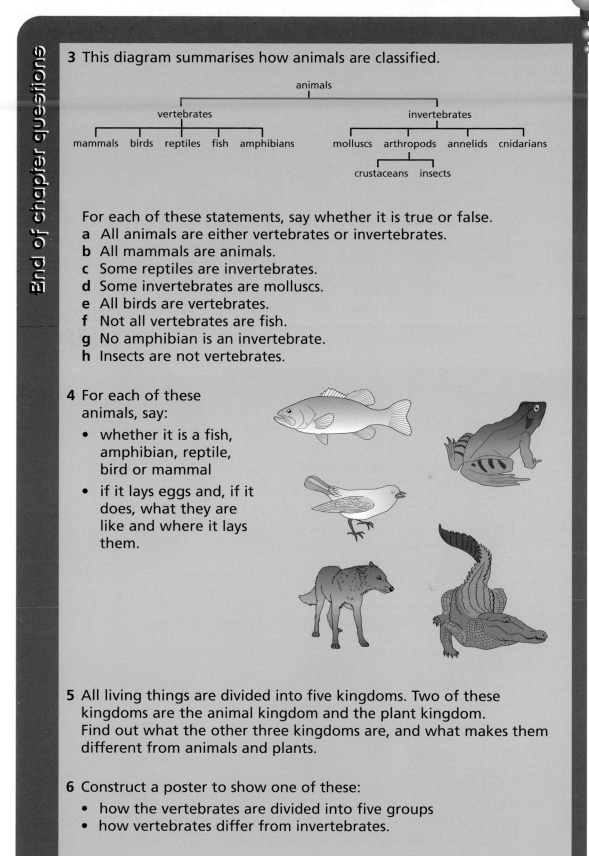

For each of these statements, say whether it is true or false.
a All animals are either vertebrates or invertebrates.
b All mammals are animals.
c Some reptiles are invertebrates.
d Some invertebrates are molluscs.
e All birds are vertebrates.
f Not all vertebrates are fish.
g No amphibian is an invertebrate.
h Insects are not vertebrates.

4 For each of these animals, say:

• whether it is a fish, amphibian, reptile, bird or mammal

• if it lays eggs and, if it does, what they are like and where it lays them.

5 All living things are divided into five kingdoms. Two of these kingdoms are the animal kingdom and the plant kingdom.
Find out what the other three kingdoms are, and what makes them different from animals and plants.

6 Construct a poster to show one of these:
• how the vertebrates are divided into five groups
• how vertebrates differ from invertebrates.

12 The Solar System and beyond

People used to believe that the Earth was flat and if we travelled too far we would fall off the edge. But when Ferdinand Magellan's expedition from 1519 to 1522 sailed all the way around the Earth and came back to where he had started from, this 'flat Earth' model was abandoned and replaced with a new one that fitted the known facts.

Don't worry we'll be OK – that flat Earth model has been replaced with a round Earth model.

In Science we use models to help us to understand and explain ideas. But we should always be looking to improve our models if new facts suggest a change is needed.

Photographs like this, taken by satellite, suggest that the 'round Earth' model is a good one.

Day and night

Although we cannot feel it, the Earth is in fact moving. It is spinning. It takes 24 hours or *one day* to turn once on its axis.

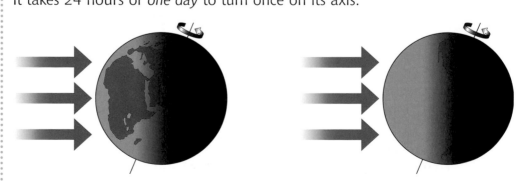

It is daytime on those parts of the Earth where there is light from the Sun. It is night time in those places that are receiving no light from the Sun.

As the Earth rotates, we move from daylight into darkness and then back into daylight.

1 Why is one day 24 hours long?

2 Draw a diagram of the Earth similar to the one shown opposite. Mark on your diagram:
   a a place where it is mid-day
   b a place where it is dawn
   c a place where it is early evening.

It is the rotation of the Earth which makes it appear that the Sun rises in the east, travels high across the southern sky and sets in the west.

Sunset. This time-lapse photograph shows the Sun setting over a city.

Sunrise. This time-lapse photograph shows the Sun rising.

Why does the Sun move across the sky? Why does the Sun always appear to rise in the east and set in the west?

In the summer, the path followed by the Sun is much higher than the path it follows in winter.

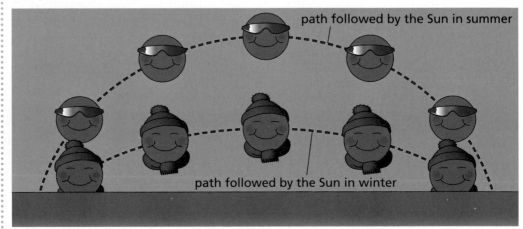

path followed by the Sun in summer

path followed by the Sun in winter

Telling the time without a watch!

Have you ever noticed how people and objects that are outside can cast a shadow? The direction and size of the shadow depends upon the position of the Sun. We can use this idea to tell the time of the day.

A sundial works by casting a shadow. As the Sun travels across the sky, the shadow cast on the dial falls in different places and you can therefore tell approximately what time it is.

Years and leap years

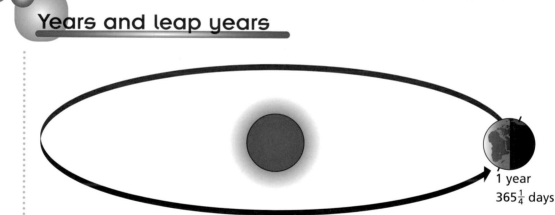

1 year
$365\frac{1}{4}$ days

As the Earth rotates it also travels around the Sun. The path it follows looks like a slightly squashed circle. It is called an **elliptical orbit**. It takes the Earth $365\frac{1}{4}$ days to complete one orbit of the Sun. This is one year.

On our calendars we show that there are 365 days in a year, but every fourth year we add the four $\frac{1}{4}$ days together and add an extra day to the year. A year which has 366 days is called a **leap year**.

3 Why is one year 365 and a quarter days long?

4 What is an elliptical orbit?

Why is there an extra day in February this year?

FEBRUARY 2004						
1	2	3	4	5	6	7
8	9	10	11	12	13	14
15	16	17	18	19	20	21
22	23	24	25	26	27	28
29						

The seasons

In Britain there are lots of changes to our climate as the Earth travels around the Sun. Each of our seasons are quite different.

Look at the four pictures below.
Which picture represents which season?

Copy and complete this table to show how the seasons affect Britain.

Season	Hours of daylight	Position of Sun in sky	Climate

This diagram will help you understand why we have these seasonal changes.

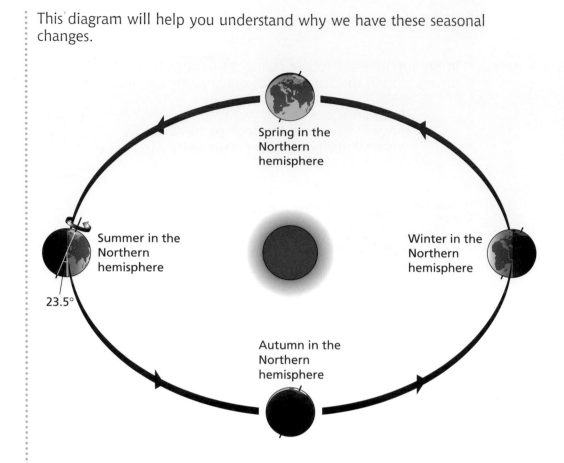

Spring in the Northern hemisphere

Summer in the Northern hemisphere

23.5°

Winter in the Northern hemisphere

Autumn in the Northern hemisphere

The axis around which the Earth spins is at an angle to the orbit it takes around the Sun. It is 'leaning over' at an angle of 23.5 degrees.

In December, the Northern hemisphere of the Earth where we live is tilted away from the Sun and we have our winter. The Southern hemisphere is tilted towards the Sun so the people there are having their summer.

In June, the Northern hemisphere is tilted towards the Sun and we in Britain have our summer. The Southern hemisphere is now tilted away from the Sun and people there are having their winter.

5 a In Australia December is in the summer, and Australians can cook their Christmas dinner outside on a barbeque. Why is this possible?

  b If a cricket team flies to Australia in the British autumn, what season is it in Australia?

  c Which way is the Earth tilted when it is spring or autumn in Britain?

To explain why the tilting of the Earth causes the seasons, we must consider how the Sun's rays warm the surface of the Earth.

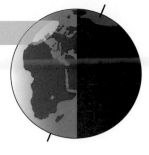

Energy from the Sun

Here the Sun's rays are spread over a large area, so each piece of land is warmed less and it feels colder. It is winter in the Northern hemisphere.

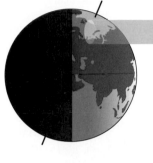

Energy from the Sun

Here the Sun's rays are spread over a smaller area, so each piece of land is warmed more and it feels warmer. It is summer in the Northern hemisphere.

YOU MAY BE ABLE TO DO WORKSHEET L1, 'HEATING EFFECT OF THE SUN'.

The Moon

An object which orbits a planet is called a **satellite**. There are two types of satellite. There are artificial or man-made satellites which we use for weather forecasting, for satellite television, etc and there are natural satellites. We have one natural satellite – it is called the Moon.

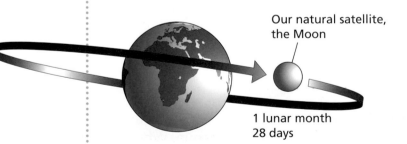

Our natural satellite, the Moon

1 lunar month
28 days

The Moon as seen from the Earth.

It takes the Moon 28 days to make one complete orbit of the Earth. The word month (moonth) originally meant a time of about 28 days. These days we call the time it takes the Moon to make one orbit of the Earth, one **lunar month**.

6 a What is a satellite?
   b Why is a month about 28 days long?

The Moon is a **non-luminous** object. It does not give out its own light. When we look at the Moon shining brightly in the night sky, we see rays of light from the Sun which have been reflected by the Moon.

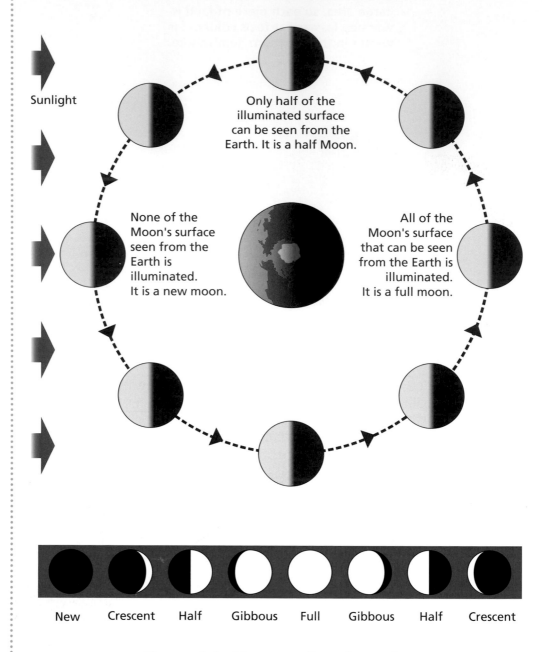

Sunlight

Only half of the illuminated surface can be seen from the Earth. It is a half Moon.

None of the Moon's surface seen from the Earth is illuminated. It is a new moon.

All of the Moon's surface that can be seen from the Earth is illuminated. It is a full moon.

| New | Crescent | Half | Gibbous | Full | Gibbous | Half | Crescent |

Phases of the Moon seen from the Earth.

As the Moon orbits the Earth the amount of light that is reflected by the Moon and which reaches the Earth, changes. This is why we see the different shapes or phases of the Moon.

Solar eclipse

The orbit of the Moon is at a slightly different angle to the orbit of the Earth. This means that occasionally, but not very often, the Moon will pass directly between the Earth and the Sun and block out the sunlight. We call this a **solar eclipse**.

The Moon is much smaller than the Sun but, because it is closer to the Earth, it can cover the whole of the Sun and block out all of the sunlight. We call this a **total eclipse**.

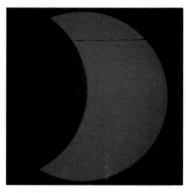

Not to scale

During a total eclipse, all of the light from the Sun is 'blocked off' by the Moon.

During a partial eclipse, part of the light from the Sun is 'blocked off' by the Moon, but not all of it.

7 The diagrams below show how the shape of the Sun appears to change during an eclipse.
Put the pictures in the right order, starting with G.

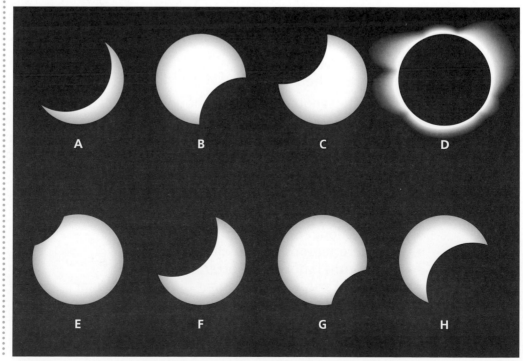

Lunar eclipse

Occasionally the Earth passes directly between the Sun and Moon. When this happens the Earth casts a shadow on the Moon.

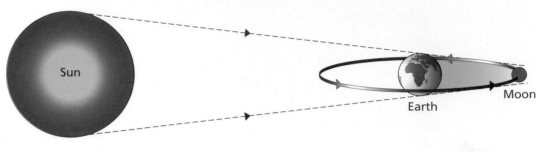

Not to scale

This is known as a **lunar eclipse**.

8 Imagine that a visitor from a distant planet arrives on the Earth for a holiday!

This visitor comes from a planet that orbits its star much more slowly than the Earth orbits the Sun.

The visitor's planet rotates on its axis much faster than the Earth does, but the planet is not tilted.

The visitor's planet also has one moon which is about the same size as the Earth's Moon, but the distance between the planet and the moon is much greater than the distance between the Earth and its Moon. The visitor's moon rotates around the planet slower than our Moon does.

Write a report home from the alien to its home planet.
Try to include these points:

* Are years longer or shorter on Earth?
* Are days longer or shorter on Earth?
* Are there seasons on the alien's planet?
* Are months longer or shorter on the Earth?
* Does the Earth's Moon appear bigger or smaller?
* Does the Earth experience solar eclipses more or less often than the visitor's planet?

The Solar System

![The Solar System diagram showing Mercury, Earth, Asteroid belt, Venus, Mars, Jupiter, Saturn, Uranus, Neptune, Pluto. Not to scale]

Our Solar System contains:

- one star we call the Sun
- nine planets that orbit the Sun together with their moons
- thousands of pieces of rock called asteroids. Most of which are found between the orbits of Mars and Jupiter.

This table contains information about the planets in our Solar System.

Planet	Distance from Sun compared with the Earth	Diameter compared with the Earth	Mass compared with the Earth	Number of moons	Day length	Year length	Average surface temperature in °C
Mercury	0.39	0.38	0.05	0	59	0.24	120
Venus	0.72	0.95	0.81	0	243	0.62	460
Earth	1	1	1	1	1	1	15
Mars	1.5	0.53	0.11	0	1	1.9	−25
Jupiter	5.2	11	318	16	0.41	11.9	−73
Saturn	10	9.5	95	22	0.44	29.5	−140
Uranus	19	4	14.5	21	0.74	84	−200
Neptune	30	3.5	17	8	0.7	165	−200
Pluto	40	0.2	0.0025	1	6.4	248	−220

Here is a mnemonic to help you remember the order of the planets from the Sun.

Many	**M**ercury
Very	**V**enus
Energetic	**E**arth
Men	**M**ars
Jogged	**J**upiter
Slowly	**S**aturn
Up to	**U**ranus
Newport	**N**eptune
Pagnell	**P**luto

9 Use the information in the table on page 179.

    a Make a list of all the planets in order of their mass, the planet with the smallest mass first.

    b Make a list of all the planets in order of their diameter, the planet with the smallest diameter first.

    c Which planet has the most moons?

    d Which planet has the shortest year?

    e Which planet has the second longest day?

    f Why is Pluto sometimes not the furthest planet from the Sun?

10 Imagine you could take a holiday touring any four planets in our Solar System. Design a holiday brochure describing the 'delights' of the planets you would visit.

Asteroids

Asteroids vary enormously in size. Some are just a few metres across, while others are several hundred kilometres in diameter. Scientists think that asteroids are the remains of a planet that broke apart. Sometimes asteroids escape from their orbit. Some of these are attracted to nearby planets and moons.

When these rocks fall to Earth they are called **meteorites**. The materials from which asteroids are made can give us clues about what is happening inside our own planet.

Ceres, the largest of the asteroids.

This meteorite crater, at Wolf Creek in the Australian desert, is 1 km across.

A meteorite crashing into the Earth can cause a lot of damage. Some scientists believe that a massive meteorite colliding with the Earth caused the mass extinction of the dinosaurs.

Life on other planets

As far as we know, the Earth is the only planet that supports life.
We believe there are three main reasons for this:

- The Earth has an atmosphere rich in oxygen.
- The Earth has water. Two thirds of the planet is covered by water.
- Most parts of the Earth have a reasonably mild temperature – between −10°C and +30°C.

If the Earth was closer to the Sun, the temperatures would be too high for life as we know it.

If the Earth was a lot further from the Sun, the temperatures would be extremely low and we would receive much less light from the Sun. As a result, most green plants could not survive here.

Is there really life out there, or are we alone?

Who or what is SETI and what do they do?

Stars

Our Sun is a star. It is brighter and bigger than the other stars we can see because it is much closer to us. In the daytime its brightness stops us from observing other stars. But at night, when Britain is facing away from the Sun, in a cloudless sky we can see thousands of stars.

Mars

Stars are luminous objects. We can see them because they give out light. Planets in the night sky are easily mistaken for stars. But planets are non-luminous objects. We see them because they reflect light from the Sun.

11 a What is the name of our nearest star?
  b Why do we only see stars at night?
  c What is the difference between a star and a planet?

The constellations

People have watched the stars in the night sky for thousands of years. They even named some of the small clusters of stars after animals, gods or objects that these patterns looked like. These patterns are called **constellations**.

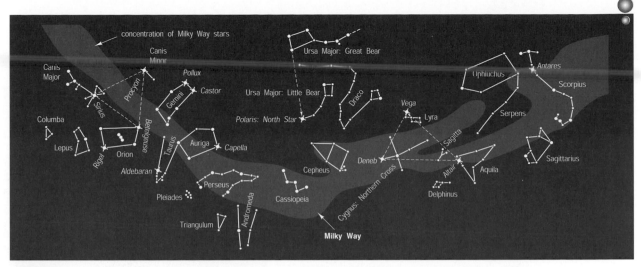

Constellations in the Milky Way seen in the Northern sky.

Can you identify any constellations in the night sky?

If you look at the stars in the evening sky and then return to look at them again some hours later, you will notice that the stars appear to have moved. They seem to have turned around or tilted a little.

In fact, the night sky is still. It is the rotation of the Earth that causes the stars to change their positions.

The Plough, part of the constellation of Ursa Major, or the Great Bear, is above the trees. It consists of seven bright stars running from upper left to lower right, to centre right.

The positions of the stars in the sky are also affected by the movement of the Earth around the Sun. The patterns of stars seen in the summer skies are slightly different to those seen in the winter skies.

12 a What is a constellation?
   b Name three constellations. Explain why the constellations were given these names.
   c Why do the stars appear to move?

The brightest star in the sky

Sirius is the brightest star in the sky. One of the reasons it appears so brightly in the night sky is that it is relatively close to Earth – 8.6 light years or 80 million million kilometres away. Sirius is twice the size of the Sun and shines around 23 times more brightly.

The name Sirius comes from the Greek word for sparkling, because the star shines so brightly. It is part of a constellation called Canis Major – the Large Dog – and, because Sirius is the brightest and largest star in this constellation,

The Canis Major constellation. At upper right is Sirius, the brightest star in the sky.

it is sometimes called the Dog Star. Sirius is accompanied by a much smaller, and therefore, fainter star known as Sirius B or the Pup Star. Although smaller, Sirius B still has a diameter of approximately 32 000 km!

Sirius is visible in the Northern hemisphere in the spring. You can find it by looking towards the south, quite low in the sky. If you can find Sirius in the night sky, you will see it flashing, often appearing to change colour. This is because the light from the star passes through the Earth's atmosphere at a much lower angle than that from other stars.

Because it contains such bright stars, Canis Major has been known to man since ancient times. According to Greek legend, Canis Major was one of the two dogs who followed the hero Orion the Hunter. This is because Canis Major is seen following the constellation of Orion across the night sky. Orion's second dog Canis Minor – the Lesser Dog – can also be seen following its master across the night sky.

Orion is said to have been killed by a scorpion's sting, and in the night sky Orion sits below the horizon, out of sight, just as the constellation Scorpio rises into view.

In ancient times, stars were extremely important in people's lives. The early Egyptians used the movement of Canis Major around the night sky as the basis for their calendar.

a Why is Sirius one of the brightest stars in the sky?

b How much brighter is Sirius compared with our Sun?

c What is the Greek word for sparkling?

d Name the Pup Star.

e Explain why the light from Sirius seems to flash and change colour.

f What do Canis Major and Canis Minor follow across the sky?

g On what did the ancient Egyptians base their calendar?

Key ideas

Now that you have completed this chapter, you should know:

- that the Earth rotates on its axis once in 24 hours – this is called a day

- that the Earth orbits the Sun once every $365\frac{1}{4}$ days – this is called a year

- that stars, like our Sun, are luminous objects – they produce their own light

- that we see the Moon and other planets only because they reflect light from the Sun to the Earth

- that the Earth's axis is tilted at an angle of 23.5 degrees – this inclination causes seasons, so when the Northern hemisphere is tilted towards the Sun, Britain experiences summer

- that solar eclipses occur when the Moon passes between Sun and the Earth

- that lunar eclipses occur when the Earth passes between the Sun and the Moon

- how, in general, the further a planet is from the Sun, the longer it takes for that planet to orbit the Sun.

Key words

asteroid	meteorite
constellation	non-luminous
ellipse	orbit
leap year	satellite
lunar eclipse	solar eclipse
lunar month	total eclipse

1 Match each of the words:

planet   asteroid   satellite   orbit   eclipse

to the following definitions.

a A small piece of an early planet.

b The total or partial disappearance of the Sun or the Moon.

c The pathway of a body around a larger body.

d A body that orbits a planet.

e A body that orbits a star and does not produce its own light.

2 Are these statements true or false ?

a The Sun appears to rise in the east and set in the west.

b Solar eclipses occur when the Earth passes between the Moon and the Sun.

c The Moon orbits the Earth once every $365\frac{1}{4}$ days.

d One year is the time that it takes for the Moon to orbit the Earth.

e The nearest planet to the Sun is Venus.

f The asteroid belt is found between Mars and Jupiter. It is the remains of an early planet ripped apart by Jupiter's massive gravitational field.

g Moons are luminous objects.

h The Moon is an artificial satellite.

i Pluto is always the furthest planet from the Sun.

j We have seasons because the Earth is spinning around.

k In summer we see different patterns of stars in the sky from those we see in the winter.

3 Copy and complete these sentences.

a One _____ lasts 24 hours. It is the time it takes for the Earth to _____ once on its axis.

b The Earth's axis is tilted at an angle of _____. It is this tilt which causes the _____ .

c When the Northern hemisphere is inclined towards the Sun, Britain experiences _____ . At this time the Southern hemisphere is tilted away from the Sun, so Australia experiences _____ .

End of chapter questions

4 Each of these statements describes an astronomical body. Rearrange the statements so that the smallest object described is first and the largest is last.

A The Sun is the Earth's nearest star. All stars are luminous objects that produce their own light.

B The Universe contains everything.

C The Moon is the Earth's natural satellite. It takes 28 days, about one month, for the Moon to orbit the Earth.

D The Solar System contains the Sun and the nine planets, their moons and the asteroids that orbit the Sun.

E The Earth is the third planet from the Sun. It takes the Earth one year to orbit the Sun.

5 Draw a poster showing the planets in the Solar System.

6 a Use the information from the table on page 179 to draw a bar graph of the masses of the nine different planets.

b Is there a connection between the distance a planet is from the Sun and the length of one year on that planet? Draw a line graph to help explain your answer.

7 Find out about the effects of the 1999 solar eclipse in Cornwall. Write a newspaper article describing this historic event.

Glossary and index